Solutions Manual to Accompany
Contract Theory

Solutions Manual to Accompany
Contract Theory

Arthur Campbell, Moshe Cohen, Florian Ederer, and Johannes Spinnewijn

For information about special quantity discounts, please email special_sales@mitpress.mit .edu

This book was set by the author.

Printed and bound in the United States of America.

Library of Congress Cataloging-in-Publication Data
Solutions manual to accompany Contract theory / Arthur Campbell ... [et al.].
    p. cm.
ISBN 978-0-262-53299-0 (pbk. : alk. paper)
1. Contracts—Methodology—Problems, exercises, etc.   I. Campbell, Arthur, Ph. D.
II. Bolton, Patrick, 1957–   Contract theory.
K840.B65 2005 Suppl.
346.0201—dc22

                                                                    2007014715

10   9   8   7   6   5   4

Contents

Preface

We would like to thank Patrick Bolton and Mathias Dewatripont for allowing us to write this book and for giving us a deeper understanding of contract theory.

Our thanks are due to Bob Gibbons, Richard Holden, Bengt Holmström, Sergei Izmalkov, Paul Klemperer and Meg Meyer for teaching us contract theory. We are grateful to our fellow graduate students at MIT and other universities, in particular Nicolas Arregui, Suman Basu, Matilde Bombardini, Dan Cao, Jesse Edgerton, Leopoldo Fergusson, Daniel Gottlieb, Raymond Guiteras, Suehyun Kwon, Jennifer La'O, Jeanne Lafortune, Jin Li, Martin Oehmke, Michael Powell, Samuel Pienknagura, Marek Pycia, Pablo Querubín, Florian Scheuer and Tom Wilkening for insightful comments and for helping us check our answers. We are also very grateful to our editor John Covell for his continuing support.

Finally, Arthur, Florian and Johannes would like to thank David Boon, Hermann Maier and Gilles De Bilde respectively for constant inspiration.

Chapter 1

Introduction

In their textbook "Contract Theory" Patrick Bolton and Mathias Dewatripont fill a critical hole in graduate economics teaching by synthesizing ideas that make up modern contract theory. We hope that this solutions manual will fill a similar gap in graduate economics teaching by allowing students and instructors to verify their answers to the exercises set by the authors.

This solutions manual follows the structure in Bolton & Dewatripont (2005) by grouping exercises into the relevant chapters. Chapters 2 to 6 start with static bilateral contracting problems such as screening, signaling and moral hazard. Chapters 7 and 8 covers the less well trodden material of multilateral contracting including auctions, bilateral trade under private information and multiagent moral hazard. Problems of repeated bilateral contracting are explored in Chapters 9 and 10. Finally, Chapters 11 to 13 cover incomplete contracts, the theory of ownership and control, contracting with externalities and common agency.

Chapter 2

Hidden Information, Screening

2.1 Question 1

Consider the following monopoly screening problem: A government agency writes a procurement contract with a firm to deliver q units of a good. The firm has constant marginal cost c, so that its profit is $P - cq$, where P denotes the payment for the transaction. The firm's cost is private information and may be either high (c_H) or low (c_L, with $0 < c_L < c_H$). The agency's prior belief about the firm's cost is $\Pr(c = c_L) = \beta$, and it makes a take-it-or-leave-it-offer to the firm (whose default profit is zero).

1. If $B(q)$ denotes the (concave) benefit to the agency of obtaining q units, what is the optimal contract for the agency?

2. Compare this second-best solution with the first-best one, obtained if costs are known by the agency. Discuss the results.

3. What would the first-best and second-best solutions be if c, instead of taking two values, were uniformly distributed on $[\underline{c}, \overline{c}]$, with $0 < \underline{c} < \overline{c}$?

2.2 Question 2

Consider the monopoly problem analyzed in section 2.1, but assume that the monopolist has one unit of the good for sale, at zero cost, while the buyer can have the following utility:

$$\theta_L - T$$

or:

$$\log(\theta_H - T).$$

The buyer's risk aversion thus rises with her valuation. Show that the seller can implement the first-best outcome (that is, sell the good for sure, leave no rents to either type of buyer, and avoid any cost of risk in equilibrium) by using a random scheme.

2.3 Question 3

A monopolist can produce a good in different qualities. The cost of producing a unit of quality s is s^2. Consumers buy at most one unit and have utility function

$$u(s|\theta) = \begin{cases} \theta s & \text{if they consume one unit of quality } s \\ 0 & \text{if they do not consume} \end{cases}$$

The monopolist decides on the quality (or qualities) it is going to produce and price. Consumers observe qualities and prices and decide which quality to buy if at all.

1. Characterize the first-best solution.

2. Suppose that the seller cannot observe θ, and suppose that

$$\theta = \begin{cases} \theta_H & \text{with probability } 1 - \beta \\ \theta_L & \text{with probability } \beta \end{cases}$$

   with $\theta_H > \theta_L > 0$. Characterize the second-best solution and consumers' informational rent.

3. Suppose now that θ is uniformly distributed on the interval $[0, 1]$. Characterize the second-best optimal quality-pricing schedule.

2.3.1 Characterization of First-Best Solution

Here we assume that the seller is perfectly informed about the buyer's characteristics. The seller can treat each type of buyer separately and offer her a type-specific contract (T_i, s_i) for each type θ_i. The seller solves the problem

$$\max_{T_i, s_i} T_i - s_i^2$$

so that

$$\theta_i s_i - T_i \geq 0.$$

Hence, differentiating with respect to s_i, yields

$$\theta_i - 2s_i = 0$$

which gives the first-best quality schedule

$$s(\theta) = \frac{1}{2}\theta.$$

2.3.2 Two Types

Using the revelation principle the seller's problem is given by

$$\max_{T_i, s_i} \beta \left[T_L - s_L^2 \right] + (1 - \beta) \left[T_H - s_H^2 \right]$$

subject to

$$
\begin{align}
\theta_L s_L - T_L &\geq 0 & \text{(IRL)} \\
\theta_H s_H - T_H &\geq 0 & \text{(IRH)} \\
\theta_L s_L - T_L &\geq \theta_L s_H - T_H & \text{(ICL)} \\
\theta_H s_H - T_H &\geq \theta_H s_L - T_L. & \text{(ICH)}
\end{align}
$$

Using the same procedure as in section 2.1.3, we can eliminate (ICL) and (IRH) and observe that (ICH) and (IRL) will bind at the optimum. Thus, the reduced unconstrained problem is

$$\max_{s_H, s_L} \beta(\theta_L s_L - s_L^2) + (1 - \beta)[\theta_H s_H - \Delta\theta s_L - s_H^2].$$

where $\Delta\theta \equiv \theta_H - \theta_L$. Differentiating with respect to s_L and s_H and accounting for the non-negativity of s, we obtain

$$
\begin{align}
s_L &= \max\left\{ \frac{1}{2}\theta_L - \frac{1 - \beta}{2\beta}\Delta\theta, 0 \right\} \\
s_H &= \frac{1}{2}\theta_H
\end{align}
$$

so that the quality for the low type is inefficiently low, but efficient for the high type. The transfers are given by

$$
\begin{align}
T_L &= \max\{\theta_L s_L, 0\} \\
T_H &= \theta_H s_H - s_L \Delta\theta.
\end{align}
$$

The informational rents are

$$
\begin{align}
u_L &= 0 \\
u_H &= s_L \Delta\theta \geq 0.
\end{align}
$$

There are no rents left to the low type, but the high type earns an informational rent as long as the low type is not excluded from the market. There may be a corner solution, where the monopolist chooses to exclude the low type, if the informational rent the monopolist has to pay becomes too large.

2.3.3 Continuum of Types

The seller's problem can be written as follows:

$$\max_{s(\theta), T(\theta)} \int_0^1 \left[T(\theta) - s(\theta)^2 \right] f(\theta) d\theta$$

subject to

$$\theta s(\theta) - T(\theta) \geq 0 \tag{IR}$$

$$\theta s(\theta) - T(\theta) \geq \theta s(\widehat{\theta}) - T(\widehat{\theta}) \text{ for all } \widehat{\theta} \in [0,1]. \tag{IC}$$

Following the implementation and optimization problems described in section 2.3.3.1 and 2.3.3.2 we can rewrite the seller's problem as

$$\max_{s(\theta)} \int_0^1 \left\{ \left[\theta s(\theta) - s(\theta)^2 \right] f(\theta) - s(\theta) \left[1 - F(\theta) \right] \right\} d\theta.$$

The first order condition yields

$$[\theta - 2s(\theta)] f(\theta) - [1 - F(\theta)] = 0.$$

Rearranging this equation we obtain

$$s(\theta) = \frac{1}{2} \left[\theta - \frac{1 - F(\theta)}{f(\theta)} \right]$$

which, using the fact that $\theta \sim U[0,1]$, simplifies to

$$s(\theta) = 0 \text{ for all } \theta < \frac{1}{2}$$
$$= \theta - \frac{1}{2} \text{ for all } \theta \geq \frac{1}{2},$$

since quality cannot be negative.

The pricing schedule is given by

$$T(\theta) = \theta s(\theta) - \int_0^\theta s(x) dx.$$

Since $s(\theta) = 0$ for $\theta < \frac{1}{2}$, $T(\theta) = 0$ for all $\theta < \frac{1}{2}$. For all $\theta \geq \frac{1}{2}$, we have

$$T(\theta) = \theta s(\theta) - \int_{\frac{1}{2}}^\theta s(x) dx$$
$$= \theta(\theta - \frac{1}{2}) - \int_{\frac{1}{2}}^\theta (x - \frac{1}{2}) dx$$
$$= \theta^2 - \frac{\theta}{2} - \frac{\theta^2}{2} + \frac{1}{8} + \frac{\theta}{2} - \frac{1}{4}$$
$$= \frac{\theta^2}{2} - \frac{1}{8}.$$

In this equilibrium, the monopolist sells only to consumers whose θ is above $\frac{1}{2}$, and thus there are efficiency losses associated with this equilibrium relative to the perfect discrimination case. Servicing low-value consumers forces the monopolist to either charge lower prices to the high types or to raise quality. Since quality is costly, the monopolist finds it profitable to shut off part of the market in order to raise the profits from the other segment of the market.

2.4   Question 4

Consider an economy with a continuum of agents who produce output q by supplying input a (for effort) with the individual production function $q = \theta a$, where θ is an idiosyncratic productivity parameter. The productivity density in the population is given by $f(\theta)$ with support $[\underline{\theta}, \bar{\theta}]$ [where $f(\theta) > \epsilon > 0$]. All agents have the same utility function $u(c) - a$, with $u' > 0$ and $u'' < 0$.

1. What is the distribution of output and consumption in the economy when all agents live and work in autarky?

2. Suppose that all agents in this economy can write an insurance contract before they know their productivity type. All agents are identical ex ante and their future productivity is i.i.d. with density $f(\theta)$. What is the optimal insurance contract when θ and a are observable ex post? What is the optimal insurance contract when only θ is observable? What is the optimal contract when neither θ nor a is observable ex post and $f(\theta)/[1 - F(\theta)]$ is monotonically increasing?

3. Interpret the last solution. Show that the marginal premium is given by

$$P'(\theta) = (\theta u'[c(\theta)] - 1)c'(\theta)$$

and $$P'(\underline{\theta}) = P'(\bar{\theta}) = 0 .$$

Discuss this solution.

2.5   Question 5

Consider an economy in which firms want to go public. A typical private firm is owned by a risk-averse entrepreneur with personal wealth W_0 and increasing, strictly concave von Neumann-Morgenstern utility function u_E. Firms are worth $\theta + \varepsilon$, where θ and ε are independent real-valued random variables. The quantity ε is realized in the future, and its realization is unknown to everybody at the time of the interaction. It has mean 0. The realization of θ, however, is known to the entrepreneur but to no one else. Assume θ can take two values, $\theta_L < \theta_H$, where θ_L occurs with probability β, and θ_H with probability $1 - \beta$. This is common knowledge, as well as the fact that $\beta\theta_L + (1 - \beta)\theta_H > 1$.

There is a monopolistic investment bank that proposes the terms of the initial public offering placed with the market. The offering is a pair $(x, T) \in [0, 1] \times \mathbb{R}^+$, where $1 - x$ is the fraction of the firm sold to the market in exchange for a payment of T to the entrepreneur. The investment bank acts as if it is risk neutral and maximizes total expected market profits from the sale:

$$U_I(x, t, \theta) = (1 - x)\theta - T$$

The safe interest rate is normalized to 0. The strategic interaction considered is the following: first, nature chooses θ, then the bank proposes the terms of the offering, and finally the entrepreneur decides about the acceptance or rejection of the offer.

1. Write down the entrepreneur's expected utility as a function of x, t, and θ.

2. Determine the first-best terms of the offering. Why will the first best not be realized in the present setting?

3. Write down the problem as a screening problem. Explain briefly.

4. Which constraints will bind at the optimum?

5. What allocation will the type-θ_L entrepreneur obtain at the optimum?

6. Solve the screening problem fully.

7. What elements of your solution are typical of screening problems? Is there anything surprising?

8. Make a conjecture for the outcome under competition between investment banks.

2.5.1   Entrepreneur's Utility

The entrepreneur is the only one who knows his type θ_i. However, like everyone else he does not know the realization of ε. The utility function of the entrepreneur with personal wealth W_0 who sold a fraction $1 - x$ of his firm in exchange for a payment of T will therefore take the expected utility form

$$Eu_E = \int u(x\,(\theta_i + \varepsilon) + T + W_0)f\,(\varepsilon)\,d\varepsilon \ .$$

2.5.2   First-Best Solution

In a first-best world, the investment bank can observe the realization of θ. The optimal contract is therefore the solution of

$$\max_{x,T}(1 - x)\theta - T$$

subject to

$$\int u(x\,(\theta + \varepsilon) + T + W_0)f\,(\varepsilon)\,d\varepsilon \geq \int u(\theta + \varepsilon + W_0)f(\varepsilon)d\varepsilon \equiv \bar{u}_\theta, \qquad (\text{IR}_\theta)$$

where $x \in [0,1]$. Notice that the outside opportunity of the entrepreneur describes his expected utility when the firm does not go public, i.e., $x = 1$ and $T = 0$. The participation constraint will always bind at the optimum, since otherwise the investment bank can lower the payment T. With one risk neutral and one risk averse player, Borch's Rule shows that the risk neutral player will bear all the risk. In this model this implies that the risk averse entrepreneur sells all his shares to the public, i.e., $x^* = 0$.

With $x^* = 0$ for the high and the low types, the first-best transfers T_H^* and T_L^* are such that

$$u(T_i^* + W_0) = \int u(\theta_i + \varepsilon + W_0)f(\varepsilon)d\varepsilon \text{ for } i = H, L.$$

Hence,

$$T_H^* > T_L^*.$$

If the investment bank cannot observe the type of the entrepreneur, the entrepreneur with the firm with the low value θ_L will always pretend to own a firm with the high value θ_H to receive the higher transfer T_H^*. Note also that

$$T_H^* < \theta_H$$
$$T_L^* < \theta_L$$

by the concavity of the utility function.

2.5.3 Second-Best Solution

We can write the problem as a screening problem in the following way

$$\max_{x_i, T_i} \beta \left[(1 - x_L)\theta_L - T_L \right] + (1 - \beta)\left[(1 - x_H)\theta_H - T_H \right]$$

subject to

$$\int u(x_L(\theta_L + \varepsilon) + T_L + W_0)f(\varepsilon)d\varepsilon \geq \bar{u}_L \qquad \text{(IRL)}$$

$$\int u(x_H(\theta_H + \varepsilon) + T_H + W_0)f(\varepsilon)d\varepsilon \geq \bar{u}_H \qquad \text{(IRH)}$$

$$\int u(x_L(\theta_L + \varepsilon) + T_L + W_0)f(\varepsilon)d\varepsilon \geq$$
$$\int u(x_H(\theta_L + \varepsilon) + T_H + W_0)f(\varepsilon)d\varepsilon \qquad \text{(ICL)}$$

$$\int u(x_H(\theta_H + \varepsilon) + T_H + W_0)f(\varepsilon)d\varepsilon \geq$$
$$\int u(x_L(\theta_H + \varepsilon) + T_L + W_0)f(\varepsilon)d\varepsilon. \qquad \text{(ICH)}$$

The conditions are very similar to the standard examples in Chapter 2. The investment bank cannot observe the type of the firm of the entrepreneur. By the revelation principle, it suffices for the bank to design contracts that are both incentive compatible and individually rational for the type for which they are designed. An important difference, however, is that the difference in quality between the two types of firms is reflected in the outside opportunity utility. That is, the minimal expected utility to be given to the entrepreneur with a high-value firm in order to convince him to go public needs to be higher than the utility for the entrepreneur with a low-value firm. The consequence is that we cannot drop the participation constraint of one of the types using the fact that the contract for this type is incentive compatible and the contract for the other type satisfies the participation constraint together with the single-crossing property. When none of the participation constraints are *a priori* slack, we cannot conclude that both participation constraints are binding and all rents are extracted from the entrepreneur no matter what his type is.

2.5.4 Binding Constraints

The first conclusion concerns the incentive compatibility constraints. The low type wants to mimic the high type when the first-best contracts are offered, whereas the high type has no incentive to mimic the low type. In order to make the low-type contract incentive compatible, the investment bank can undertake two actions. The first one is to introduce extra risk in the payoff of the high type by increasing x_H and reducing T_H. The second action is to increase T_L and allow some rents to the low type. The increase in risk increases the risk premium to be paid to the high type, but the high-type contract becomes relatively less attractive to the low type compared to the high type, given the lower value θ determining the income from the shares in the firm. As will be discussed later on, the crucial trade-off facing the investment bank is between the rent extraction of the low type and the risk premium given to the high type. In any case (ICL) will be binding, but (ICH) will not. In fact, using $x_L^{**} = 0$, we can show that the satisfaction of (ICH) is always implied by the single-crossing property and (ICL) being binding. First note that

$$\int u(x_H\left(\theta_H + \varepsilon\right) + T_H + W_0)f\left(\varepsilon\right)d\varepsilon > \int u(x_H\left(\theta_L + \varepsilon\right) + T_H + W_0)f\left(\varepsilon\right)d\varepsilon$$

since $\theta_H > \theta_L$. Now since (ICL) is binding we have

$$\int u(x_H\left(\theta_L + \varepsilon\right) + T_H + W_0)f\left(\varepsilon\right)d\varepsilon = \int u(x_L\left(\theta_L + \varepsilon\right) + T_L + W_0)f\left(\varepsilon\right)d\varepsilon.$$

Finally, since $x_L^{**} = 0$ we have

$$\int u(x_L\left(\theta_L + \varepsilon\right) + T_L + W_0)f\left(\varepsilon\right)d\varepsilon = \int u(x_L\left(\theta_H + \varepsilon\right) + T_L + W_0)f\left(\varepsilon\right)d\varepsilon$$

and so (ICH) is always satisfied.

The second conclusion is that (IRH) will be binding with certainty. As long as (IRH) is not binding, the principal can decrease the payment T_H and increase his own payoff. Moreover, the binding (ICL) will be relaxed, while the left-hand side of the slack (ICH) will decrease.

2.5.5 Low-Type Allocation

The entrepreneur with a low-value firm would like to pretend to have a firm with higher value to receive a higher payment when going public. A possible remedy is to increase the payment to the low-value firms. However, there is still no reason not to take all the risk away from the entrepreneur with the low-value firm. An increase in risk would increase the risk premium due to the entrepreneur or increase the incentive to pretend to have a high-value firm. Therefore, the share of the entrepreneur in his low type firm will be zero, as it was in the efficient contract, that is

$$x_L^{**} = x_L^* = 0.$$

The payment T_L^{**} will be bounded by T_L^* and T_H^*, the specific level will depend on the trade-off between the rent extraction from the low type and the risk premium claimed by the high type.

2.5.6 Full Screening Problem

Using the previous observations, the screening problem can be reduced to

$$\max_{x_H, T_H, T_L} - \beta T_L + (1 - \beta) \left[(1 - x_H) \theta_H - T_H \right]$$

subject to

$$u(T_L + W_0) \geq \bar{u}_L \tag{IRL}$$

$$\int u(x_H (\theta_H + \varepsilon) + T_H + W_0) f(\varepsilon) \, d\varepsilon = \bar{u}_H \tag{IRH}$$

$$u(T_L + W_0) = \int u(x_H (\theta_L + \varepsilon) + T_H + W_0) f(\varepsilon) \, d\varepsilon. \tag{ICL}$$

Denote by $\lambda_L, \lambda_H,$ and μ the Lagrange multiplier on (IRL), (IRH), and (ICL) respectively. The first order conditions are

$$\frac{\partial \mathcal{L}}{\partial x_H} = 0 \Leftrightarrow$$

$$(1 - \beta) \theta_H = \lambda_H \int u'(x_H (\theta_H + \varepsilon) + T_H + W_0) [\theta_H + \varepsilon] f(\varepsilon) \, d\varepsilon$$

$$- \mu \int u'(x_H (\theta_L + \varepsilon) + T_H + W_0) [\theta_L + \varepsilon] f(\varepsilon) \, d\varepsilon$$

$$\frac{\partial \mathcal{L}}{\partial T_H} = 0 \Leftrightarrow$$

$$(1 - \beta) = \lambda_H \int u'(x_H (\theta_H + \varepsilon) + T_H + W_0) f(\varepsilon) \, d\varepsilon$$

$$- \mu \int u'(x_H (\theta_L + \varepsilon) + T_H + W_0) f(\varepsilon) \, d\varepsilon$$

$$\frac{\partial \mathcal{L}}{\partial T_L} = 0 \Leftrightarrow$$

$$\beta = (\lambda_L + \mu)\, u'(T_L + W_0).$$

2.5.7   Discussion

The first order conditions are difficult to interpret, but we can distinguish between two important cases, that is whether the (IRL) will bind or not.

Case 1: $T_L^{**} = T_L^*$

If $\lambda_L > 0$, the (IRL) will bind, thus $T_L^{**} = T_L^*$. In this case, the x_H^{**} is increased above $x_H^{**} = 0$, while T_H^{**} is reduced to extract all rents, given that (IRH) is binding, from the high type until the low type has no more incentive to choose the high-type contract. More formally,

$$u(T_L^{**} + W_0) = u(T_L^* + W_0)$$

$$\int u(x_H^{**}(\theta_H + \varepsilon) + T_H^{**} + W_0) f(\varepsilon)\, d\varepsilon = u(T_H^* + W_0)$$

$$\int u(x_H^{**}(\theta_L + \varepsilon) + T_H^{**} + W_0) f(\varepsilon)\, d\varepsilon = u(T_L^* + W_0).$$

Case 2: $T_L^{**} > T_L^*$

Although the investment bank can extract all rents from both types in the first case, it must pay a risk premium to the high type, since it introduces extra risk in his payoff. Therefore, the investment bank could be better off by giving some rents to the low type in order to reduce the risk premium paid to the high type. Hence the (IRL) will not bind, $\lambda_L = 0$ and $T_L^{**} \geq T_L^*$. The second case is more likely to occur when β is low and the risk aversion is high. Notice that for very low values for β we cannot even exclude a pooling equilibrium where both types are offered $(x, T) = (0, T_H^*)$. The effect of the difference in quality $\theta_H - \theta_L$ is ambiguous, since a higher difference increases the difference in first-best transfers $T_H^* - T_L^*$, so it increases the incentive to mimic the high type, but it also makes the introduction of risk more effective to take away this incentive. As in the standard screening examples, distortions can occur in the allocation given to the type who would otherwise be mimicked, and, as always, no rents are given to this type. The rents given to the other type will depend on the risk premium that has to be paid because of the inefficient allocation. A special feature of this model is that it can be optimal to give no rents to both types without excluding one of them.

2.5.8   Competition

Under perfect competition between investment banks, either the least-cost separating equilibrium will occur or no equilibrium exists. The optimal contracts solve

$$\max_{x_i, T_i} \beta \int u(x_L (\theta_L + \varepsilon) + T_L + W_0) f(\varepsilon) \, d\varepsilon + (1 - \beta) \int u(x_H (\theta_H + \varepsilon) + T_H + W_0) f(\varepsilon) \, d\varepsilon$$

subject to

$$\beta \left[(1 - x_L) \theta_L - T_L \right] + (1 - \beta) \left[(1 - x_H) \theta_H - T_H \right] = 0$$

and the (ICL) and (ICH).

Based on the previous discussion, it is clear that in the least-cost separating equilibrium $\hat{x}_L = 0$, but $\hat{x}_H > 0$ in order to satisfy the (ICL). $\hat{T}_L$ and $\hat{T}_H$ are set to increase expected utility and to extract all profits from the investment banks. However, if the proportion of low-types β is low, this contract may be dominated by a pooling contract with $x = 0$ and $T = \beta\theta_L + (1 - \beta)\theta_H$ for both types. Due to cream-skimming, however, this pooling contract cannot be an equilibrium.

Chapter 3

Hidden Information, Signaling

3.1 Question 6

Consider a firm that can invest an amount I in a project generating high observable cash flow $C > 0$ with probability θ and 0 otherwise: $\theta \in \{\theta_L, \theta_H\}$ with $\theta_H - \theta_L \equiv \Delta > 0$ and $\Pr[\theta = \theta_L] = \beta$. The firm needs to raise I from external investors who do not observe the value of θ. Assume that $\theta_L C - I > 0$. Everybody is risk neutral and there is no discounting.

1. Suppose that the firms can only promise to repay an amount R chosen by the firm (with $0 \le R \le C$) when cash flow is C and 0 otherwise. Can a good firm signal its type?

2. Suppose now that the firm also has the possibility of pledging some assets as collateral for the loan: Should a "default" occur (the firm being unable to repay R), an asset of value K to the firm is transferred to the creditor whose valuation is xK with $0 < x < 1$. The size of the collateral K is a choice variable. Give a necessary and sufficient condition for the "best" Perfect Bayesian Equilibrium to be separating. How does it depend on β and x? Explain.

3.2 Question 7

Consider the following modification of the Myers-Majluf (1984) model. Suppose that the asset in place can take three ex post values, $A = 0, 1, 2$, and let $\gamma = \text{Prob}(A = 1)$ and $\mu = \text{Prob}(A = 2)$. The new project, however, has a safe value $V_N > I$, where I is the start-up cost of the new project. Suppose that the firm can be of two different types, G and B, where $(\gamma, \mu) \in \{(\gamma_B, \mu_B), (\gamma_G, \mu_G)\}$, with $\gamma_G > \gamma_B$, but

$$E[A_G] \equiv \gamma_G + 2\mu_G = \gamma_B + 2\mu_B \equiv E[A_B]$$

Solve for the set of perfect Bayesian Equilibria under, respectively, equity financing and debt financing. Discuss.

3.3   Question 8

A firm has a project requiring an investment of 20 at $t = 0$ for a sure return of 30 at $t = 1$. There is no discounting. The investment cost has to be raised from the financial market. Assume that a new equity issue is proposed. Potential new investors are uncertain about the value of the firm's assets in place: $A \in \{50, 100\}$ with $\Pr[A = 100] = 0.1$.

1. Suppose that investors believe that both types of firms invest. What fraction of the firm's equity has to be issued to new investors? What are the payoffs to existing shareholders if they undertake the project? Are these beliefs reasonable?

2. Suppose that investors believe that only bad firms issue new equity. Same questions.

3. Suppose now that shareholders commit at $t = 0$ to a wasteful advertising campaign at $t = 1$ after the project return is realized. The advertising expenditure is an irreversible action on the part of the firm that results in a drop in profits of K. The size of the expenditure is a choice variable. Show that a good firm can signal its type through such expenditures. Discuss.

3.3.1   Both Types Invest

Both types invest, so pooling gives $\frac{20}{0.1 \times 100 + 0.9 \times 50 + 30} = \frac{20}{85}$ (share of 20 over the expected value). Existing shareholders in the good firm in expectation obtain

$$\frac{65}{85} \times (30 + 100) = 99.41.$$

However, otherwise the shareholders could get 100. So it is not reasonable for them to invest.

Existing shareholders in the bad firm receive

$$\frac{65}{85} \times (30 + 50) = 61.1.$$

Otherwise they could get 50, so beliefs are unreasonable overall since it only makes sense for the bad types to invest, but not for both.

3.3.2 Only Bad Firms Invest

Given the new formulation, they then sell a fraction $\frac{20}{80} = 0.25$ of the firm. Bad firms now obtain

$$\frac{3}{4} \times 80 = 60$$

whereas before they got 50. The good firms would have to issue even a higher fraction of equity. So, the beliefs are reasonable.

3.3.3 Wasteful Advertising

In period $t = 0$ the firm commits to a wasteful advertising campaign at $t = 1$ after the return is realized. Profits decrease by K. If we know the firm is a good type, the share is equal to $\frac{20}{130-K}$. The shareholders obtain

$$\frac{110 - K}{130 - K} \times (130 - K) = 110 - K.$$

High types signal their share by advertising. Beliefs are such that with no advertising firms are thought to be of a low type.

So without advertising they need to sell 25% of the firm, which means that good firms would obtain

$$0.75 \times 130 = \frac{390}{4} < 100.$$

With advertising there will be a cutoff value where the bad firm's incentive compatibility constraint will bind

$$
\begin{aligned}
\left(1 - \frac{20}{130 - K}\right)(80 - K) &\leq 60 \\
8800 - 190K + K^2 &\leq 7800 - 60K \\
K^2 - 130K + 1000 &\leq 0.
\end{aligned}
$$

This yields the relevant cutoff value for K given by $K^* = 8.21$. So, for example if $K = 8.5$, the high firm still makes a positive profit, but a deviation by the low firm will give it

$$\left(1 - \frac{20}{130 - 8.5}\right)(80 - 8.5) = 59.730 < 60$$

and

$$\left(1 - \frac{20}{130 - 8.5}\right)(130 - 8.5) = 101.5 > 100.$$

Hence, we obtain separation. The reason this works is that the good firm benefits more from a decrease in the share of the equity it has to give outsiders (since it is more profitable), and thus can use the advertising as a signal. Note however that this is wasteful advertising which, similar to money burning, is a costly signaling mechanism which must be used by the high-value firm. For a comparison see Milgrom & Roberts (1986).

3.4 Question 9

Consider a two-period model with no discounting. An entrepreneur has a project generating a random cash flow $C \in \{\underline{C}, \overline{C}\}$ at $t = 1$ where $\overline{C} - \underline{C} \equiv \Delta > 0$ and $\Pr\left[C = \overline{C}\right] \equiv \theta$. The (project) type $\theta \in \{\theta_L, \theta_H\}$, with $\theta_H > \theta_L$, is the entrepreneur's private information, and the (common knowledge) market prior is $\Pr\left[\theta = \theta_L\right] \equiv \beta$. The project requires an investment I at $t = 0$ that the entrepreneur needs to raise from the (competitive) market. Assume that $\underline{C} + \theta_L \Delta > I > \underline{C}$. The entrepreneur is assumed to be restricted to issuing debt only or equity only.

1. Show that there exist perfect Bayesian equilibria in which both types issue debt. Which one among these equilibria is preferred by θ_H entrepreneurs? Show that there may exist perfect Bayesian equilibria in which both types issue equity. Which one among these equilibria is preferred by θ_H entrepreneurs? And do θ_H entrepreneurs prefer this equilibrium to their most preferred debt equilibrium? Explain.

2. In the remainder of the problem, assume that the entrepreneur incurs a nonpecuniary cost of financial distress $K > 0$ whenever she is unable to meet a repayment at $t = 1$. Give conditions on K for a pooling equilibrium with debt to exist. Give conditions on K for a separating equilibrium to exist. Can θ_H entrepreneurs be better off with $K > 0$ than with $K = 0$ (in their preferred equilibrium)?

3.4.1 No Costs of Financial Distress

We have the following relationship

$$\underline{C} + \theta_L \Delta > I > \underline{C}$$

so investment in the project is profitable for both types.

We first consider separating equilibria that include equity only. Let x_H and x_L denote the respective repayment shares of the two types. We have the following constraints that guarantee investor repayment

$$(1 - \theta_L)x_L\underline{C} + \theta_L x_L\overline{C} \geq I$$
$$(1 - \theta_H)x_H\underline{C} + \theta_H x_H\overline{C} \geq I.$$

Clearly, the low firm would always want to deviate, since the high firm has to offer a lower share, so no separating equilibrium is possible.

Now consider pooling equilibria with equity so both types offer a share x. We can have pooling if

$$[\beta\theta_L + (1 - \beta)\theta_H]\, x\overline{C} + [\beta(1 - \theta_L) + (1 - \beta)(1 - \theta_H)]x\underline{C} \geq I.$$

Clearly, both types prefer the least-cost pooling contract, that is the pooling contract with the lowest x which still satisfies the above inequality. For this equilibrium we obtain the following equilibrium share:

$$x = \frac{I}{[\beta\theta_L + (1-\beta)\theta_H]\overline{C} + [\beta(1-\theta_L) + (1-\beta)(1-\theta_H)]\underline{C}}.$$

We now consider debt contracts. In debt contracts we specify a repayment R which is the "face value of the debt." The investor gets $\min\{R, C\}$. In our case, both types use the same payment in the low realization, i.e., $R_L = \underline{C}$. A pooling equilibrium must satisfy the following relation:

$$[\beta\theta_L + (1-\beta)\theta_H]R + [\beta(1-\theta_L) + (1-\beta)(1-\theta_H)]\underline{C} \geq I,$$

where R denotes the debt payment in the high state. Again, the most preferred equilibrium is that with the lowest possible R. As a result we have

$$R = \frac{I - [\beta(1-\theta_L) + (1-\beta)(1-\theta_H)]\underline{C}}{\beta\theta_L + (1-\beta)\theta_H}.$$

Now, to show that debt is preferred to equity consider the following deviation argument. Consider a contract that specifies a (different) equity share for both the high and low realization, x_L and x_H respectively. Thus the individual rationality constraint of the investors is

$$x_H[\beta\theta_L + (1-\beta)\theta_H]\overline{C} + x_L[\beta(1-\theta_L) + (1-\beta)(1-\theta_H)]\underline{C} = I.$$

Next consider trading the equity share in the high realization for that in the low realization

$$\frac{dx_H}{dx_L} = -\frac{\beta\theta_L + (1-\beta)\theta_H}{\beta(1-\theta_L) + (1-\beta)(1-\theta_H)}\frac{\overline{C}}{\underline{C}}.$$

Finally, consider the good entrepreneurs. They are getting

$$[1-x_H]\overline{C}\theta_H + [1-x_L]\underline{C}(1-\theta_H)$$

and thus they would trade at the lower rate of

$$\frac{dx_H}{dx_L} = -\frac{\theta_H}{(1-\theta_H)}\frac{\overline{C}}{\underline{C}}.$$

Thus it is clear that the entrepreneurs would be more willing to give up equity in the low state and will do so until $x_L = 1$, i.e., until they give up all of their share of equity in the low state, which reduces the contract into a debt contract. The reason for this preference is that with the debt contract, which forces the bad entrepreneurs to pay their entire cash flow in the bad state, the total cross subsidy is reduced.

3.4.2   Costs of Financial Distress

The new assumption that the cost of financial distress, K, is positive, helps since now imitation of the high types entails the cost of a high probability of financial distress. For pooling in debt to exist we need low types and high types not to prefer equity. We shall assume that off-equilibrium beliefs are such that only low types issue equity. So we need to check whether high types and low types will want to deviate from the pooling to equity. However, the high type should not want to deviate, since we showed above that they prefer the debt pooling to the equity pooling, and the off-equilibrium beliefs specified make equity even less attractive than in the pooling scenario (since here the share assumes only low types issue equity).

Pooling with debt yields the following equilibrium values for R and x, given the above beliefs

$$R^{pool} = \frac{I - [\beta(1 - \theta_L) + (1 - \beta)(1 - \theta_H)]\underline{C}}{\beta\theta_L + (1 - \beta)\theta_H}$$

$$x = \frac{I}{\theta_L\overline{C} + (1 - \theta_L)\underline{C}}.$$

Hence, K must satisfy the following conditions. For the low type we have

$$(1 - \theta_L)(-K) + \theta_L(\overline{C} - R) \geq (1 - x)[\theta_L\overline{C} + (1 - \theta_L)\underline{C})].$$

From this expression we obtain that

$$K \leq \frac{\theta_L(\overline{C} - R) - (1 - x)[\theta_L\overline{C} + (1 - \theta_L)\underline{C})]}{1 - \theta_L}.$$

For the high type, the following condition must hold:

$$(1 - \theta_H)(-K) + \theta_H(\overline{C} - R) \geq (1 - x)[\theta_H\overline{C} + (1 - \theta_H)\underline{C})].$$

Rearranging, we obtain

$$K \leq \frac{\theta_H(\overline{C} - R) - (1 - x)[\theta_H\overline{C} + (1 - \theta_H)\underline{C})]}{1 - \theta_H}.$$

But as mentioned, this is implied, given the analysis above.

Now for a separating equilibrium to exist, the low type chooses to issue equity whereas the high type chooses debt. As a result the following set of inequalities must hold

$$\theta_H(\overline{C} - R) + (1 - \theta_H)(-K) \geq (1 - x)[\theta_H\overline{C} + (1 - \theta_H)\underline{C})]$$
$$(1 - x)[\theta_L\overline{C} + (1 - \theta_L)\underline{C})] \geq \theta_L(\overline{C} - R) + (1 - \theta_L)(-K)$$

where the values for R and x are now given by

$$R^{sep} = \overline{C} - \frac{I}{\theta_H}$$

$$x = \frac{I}{\theta_L\overline{C} + (1 - \theta_L)\underline{C}}.$$

Combining the two inequalities we can find conditions on K for which a separating equilibrium exists:

$$K_L \leq K \leq K_H$$

where

$$K_L \equiv \frac{\theta_L(\overline{C} - R) - (1-x)[\theta_L\overline{C} + (1-\theta_L)\underline{C})]}{1 - \theta_L}$$

$$K_H \equiv \frac{\theta_H(\overline{C} - R) - (1-x)[\theta_H\overline{C} + (1-\theta_H)\underline{C})]}{1 - \theta_H}.$$

The high type prefers a separating equilibrium with positive costs of financial costs to a debt pooling equilibrium (which is preferred to an equity pooling equilibrium) if and only if

$$\theta_H(\overline{C} - R^{sep}) + (1-\theta_H)(-K) \geq \theta_H(\overline{C} - R^{pool}).$$

where R^{pool} is defined as in part 1. Rearranging we obtain a condition on K

$$K \leq \frac{a + \theta_H}{a(1 - \theta_H)} I - \frac{\theta_H}{1 - \theta_H}\left(\overline{C} + \frac{b}{a}\underline{C}\right),$$

where

$$a = \beta\theta_L + (1 - \beta)\theta_H$$
$$b = \beta(1 - \theta_L) + (1 - \beta)(1 - \theta_H).$$

The high type also prefers a separating equilibrium with positive K to an equity pooling equilibrium if and only if

$$\theta_H(\overline{C} - R^{sep}) + (1 - \theta_H)(-K) \geq (1 - x^{pool})\left[\theta_H\overline{C} + (1 - \theta_H)\underline{C}\right],$$

where x^{pool} is as defined above in part 1. Rearranging we obtain another condition on K

$$K \leq \frac{I(s + \widetilde{\theta}_H) - \widetilde{\theta}_H}{s(1 - \theta_H)}$$

where

$$s = a\overline{C} + b\underline{C}$$
$$\widetilde{\theta}_H = \theta_H\overline{C} + (1 - \theta_H)\underline{C}.$$

Thus, for small positive K the θ_H types will prefer a separating equilibrium with a cost of financial distress to a pooling equilibrium in both debt and equity without such costs. A small increase in K allows a separation which makes θ_H types better off.

Chapter 4

Hidden Action, Moral Hazard

4.1 Question 10

Take a standard moral-hazard problem where the principal considers offering the agent a lottery rather than a fixed payment w_i if output q_i is observed. Specifically, the agent would receive in this case w_{ij} with probability $p_{ij} \geq 0$, with $j = 1, 2, ..., m$ and

$$\sum_{j=1}^{m} p_{ij} = 1$$

Assume the agent's utility function is $u(w) - \psi(a)$. Show that such a randomizing incentive scheme cannot be optimal if the principal is risk neutral and the agent is strictly risk averse.

4.1.1 Randomizing Scheme Cannot Be Optimal

The problem of the risk neutral principal is:

$$\max_{\{w_{ij}\}} \sum_i \pi_i (a) \left(q_i - \sum_j p_{ij} w_{ij} \right)$$

subject to

$$\sum_i \pi_i (a) \left(\sum_j p_{ij} u (w_{ij}) \right) - \psi (a) \geq \overline{u} \qquad \text{(IR)}$$

$$a \in \arg\max_{\tilde{a}} \sum_i \pi_i (\tilde{a}) \left(\sum_j p_{ij} u (w_{ij}) \right) - \psi (\tilde{a}) . \qquad \text{(IC)}$$

Assume that a non-degenerate contract $\{w_{ij}^*\}$ that pays w_{ij} with strictly positive probability p_{ij} (where i indexes the output realization q_i) is optimal. Now consider a contract that pays constant w_i when any q_i is realized such that

$$u(w_i) = \sum_j p_{ij} u(w_{ij}).$$

This contract leaves both the (IR) and (IC) constraints unaffected. However, for a strictly risk averse agent the expected utility of the initial randomizing scheme is smaller than the utility of the expected value of this scheme,

$$u(w_i) = \sum_j p_{ij} u(w_{ij}) < u\left(\sum_j p_{ij} w_{ij}\right).$$

Hence, the contract paying a constant w_i for all q_i decreases the expected wage bill for the risk neutral principal, given $w_i < \sum_j p_{ij} w_{ij}$. This contract therefore improves on the initial contract so that the latter cannot be optimal.

4.2   Question 11

Consider a risk-averse individual [with utility function of money $u(.)$] with initial wealth W_0 who faces the risk of having an accident and losing an amount x of her wealth. She has access to a perfectly competitive market of risk-neutral insurers who can offer schedules $R(x)$ of repayments net of the insurance premium. Assume that the distribution of x, which depends on accident-prevention effort a, has an atom at $x = 0$: $f(0, a) = 1 - p(a)$ and $f(x, a) = p(a)g(x)$ for $x > 0$. Assume $p''(a) > 0 > p'(a)$. The individual's (increasing and convex) cost of effort, separable from her utility of money, is $\psi(a)$. Determine the first-best and second-best insurance contracts. Discuss.

4.3   Question 12

Consider a principal-agent problem with three exogenous states of nature, $\theta_1, \theta_2,$ and θ_3; two effort levels, a_L and a_H; and two output levels, distributed as follows as a function of the state of nature and the effort level:

State of nature	θ_1	θ_2	θ_3
Probability	0.25	0.5	0.25
Output under a_H	18	18	1
Output under a_L	18	1	1

The principal is risk neutral while the agent has utility function $\sqrt{w}$ when receiving monetary compensation w, minus the cost of effort, which is normalized to 0 for a_L and to 0.1 for a_H. The agent's reservation expected utility is 0.1.

1. Derive the first-best contract.

2. Derive the second-best contract when only output levels are observable.

3. Assume the principal can buy for a price of 0.1 an information system that allows the parties to verify whether state of nature θ_3 happened or not. Will the principal buy this information system? Discuss.

4.4 Question 13

Consider the modified linear managerial-incentive-scheme problem, where the manager's effort, a affects current profits, $q_1 = a + \varepsilon_{q_1}$, and future profits, $q_2 = a + \varepsilon_{q_2}$, where ε_{q_t} are i.i.d. with normal distribution $N(0, \sigma_q^2)$. The manager retires at the end of the first period, and the manager's compensation cannot be based on q_2. However, her compensation can depend on the stock price $P = 2a + \varepsilon_P$, where $\varepsilon_P \sim N(0, \sigma_P^2)$. Derive the optimal compensation contract $t = w + fq_1 + sP$. Discuss how it depends on σ_P^2 and on its relation with σ_q^2. Compare your solution with that in the Chapter.

4.4.1 CEO Compensation

Note that this question uses notation that is not consistent with the exposition in section 4.6.1. The program for this problem is the following,

$$\max_{a,w,f,s} E\left(q_1 + q_2 - t\right)$$

subject to

$$E\left(-e^{-\eta[t-\psi(a)]}\right) \geq -e^{-\eta\bar{t}} \qquad \text{(IR)}$$

$$a \in \arg\max_{\hat{a}} E\left(-e^{-\eta[t-\psi(\hat{a})]}\right) \qquad \text{(IC)}$$

$$t = w + fq_1 + sP$$

$\Leftrightarrow$

$$\max_{a,w,f,s} 2a - (w + fa + 2sa)$$

subject to

$$w + fa + 2sa - \frac{\eta}{2}\left(f^2\sigma_q^2 + s^2\sigma_P^2 + 2sf\sigma_{qP}\right) - \frac{c}{2}a^2 \geq \bar{t}$$

$$a \in \arg\max_{\hat{a}} w + f\hat{a} + 2s\hat{a} - \frac{\eta}{2}\left(f^2\sigma_q^2 + s^2\sigma_P^2 + 2sf\sigma_{qP}\right) - \frac{c}{2}\hat{a}^2.$$

We can apply the first-order approach and substitute the first order condition

$$a = \frac{f + 2s}{c}$$

for the incentive compatibility constraint. Introducing this efficient level of effort and substituting the outside opportunity level plus the risk premium plus the cost of effort for the wage, we obtain

$$\max_{f,s} 2\frac{f + 2s}{c} - \frac{\eta}{2}\left(f^2\sigma_q^2 + s^2\sigma_P^2 + 2sf\sigma_{qP}\right) - \frac{(f + 2s)^2}{2c} - \bar{t}.$$

The first order conditions with respect to f and s are respectively

$$\frac{2}{c} - \eta\left(f^*\sigma_q^2 + s^*\sigma_{qP}\right) - \frac{f^* + 2s^*}{c} = 0$$

$$\frac{4}{c} - \eta\left(s^*\sigma_P^2 + f^*\sigma_{qP}\right) - 2\frac{f^* + 2s^*}{c} = 0.$$

After some rewriting, the equations become

$$f^* = \frac{2 - s^*(2 + \eta c\sigma_{qP})}{1 + \eta c\sigma_q^2}$$

$$f^* = \frac{2 - s^*(2 + \frac{\eta c\sigma_P^2}{2})}{1 + \frac{\eta c\sigma_{qP}}{2}},$$

and we finally find

$$f^* = \frac{\sigma_P^2 - 2\sigma_{qP}}{2\sigma_q^2 + \frac{\sigma_P^2}{2} - 2\sigma_{qP} + \frac{\eta c}{2}(\sigma_P^2\sigma_q^2 - \sigma_{qP}^2)}$$

$$s^* = \frac{2\sigma_q^2 - \sigma_{qP}}{2\sigma_q^2 + \frac{\sigma_P^2}{2} - 2\sigma_{qP} + \frac{\eta c}{2}(\sigma_P^2\sigma_q^2 - \sigma_{qP}^2)}.$$

4.4.2 Comparison

Compared to the example in Chapter 4, the importance of the agent's effort has doubled for the principal. Among the contractible variables, only the impact of a change in effort on the stock price has doubled. Although the agent's effort now determines the output in two periods, the output in the second period is not contractible. The stock price therefore becomes a more precise indicator of effort than the contractible output. If we consider the relative size of the incentives at the optimum

$$\frac{f^*}{s^*} = \frac{\sigma_P^2 - 2\sigma_{qP}}{2\sigma_q^2 - \sigma_{qP}}$$

and compare this to the equivalent ratio in Chapter 4[1]

$$\frac{f^*}{s^*} = \frac{\sigma_P^2 - \sigma_{qP}}{\sigma_q^2 - \sigma_{qP}},$$

---

[1] In section 4.6.1 f and s and w and t are interchanged.

we notice that the principal puts relatively more weight on the stock prices. This weight is exactly double when both indicators are independent, $\sigma_{qP} = 0$.

4.5 Question 14

Consider the following principal-agent problem. There is a project whose probability of success is a (a is also the effort made by the risk-neutral agent, at cost a^2). In case of success the return is R, and in case of failure the return is 0. The parameter R can take two values, X with probability λ and 1 with probability $1 - \lambda$. To undertake the project, the agent needs to borrow an amount I from the principal. The sequence of events is as follows:

- First, the principal offers the agent a debt contract, with face value D_0. The agent accepts or rejects this contract.

- Second, nature determines the value R that would occur in case of success. This value is observed by both principal and agent. The principal can then choose to lower the debt from D_0 to D_1.

- The agent chooses a level of effort a. This level is not observed by the principal.

- The project succeeds or not. If the project succeeds, the agent pays the minimum of R and the face value of debt D_1.

Answer the following questions:

1. Compute the subgame-perfect equilibrium of this game as a function of I, λ, and X.

2. When do we have $D_1 < D_0$? Discuss.

4.6 Question 15

An entrepreneur has two projects available, each requiring an investment outlay of 6 at $t = 0$. The first project generates cash flow $C_1 \in \{5, 45\}$ at $t = 1$. The second project generates cash flow $C_2 \in \{0, 48\}$. The probability of getting a high cash flow is in each case equal to a, where a also denotes the level of effort of the entrepreneur. The entrepreneur has cost of effort of $40a^2$ and can choose between three effort levels: $a \in \{0, \frac{1}{3}, \frac{1}{2}\}$. The firm has no assets in place. Everybody is risk neutral, and there is no discounting. The two projects are mutually exclusive.

1. If the entrepreneur can self-finance, what level of effort will she choose under each project? Which project is worth investing in?

2. Suppose now that the entrepreneur is cash constrained and that the project is entirely financed with debt. What face value D of debt should the entrepreneur choose under each project? Which project does she end up choosing if she can get an unconditional loan, that is, a loan that does not depend on which of the two projects she decides to invest in? Discuss.

3. Can the entrepreneur do better by issuing a fraction s of equity instead of financing the project with debt?

4.6.1 Self-Financing

Project 1

If the entrepreneur can self-finance, she will choose her effort level satisfying

$$\max_a 45a + 5(1 - a) - 40a^2$$

$\Leftrightarrow$

$$\max_a a - a^2.$$

Hence,

$$a_1^* = \frac{1}{2} \text{ and } Eu_1(\frac{1}{2}) = \frac{1}{2} \times 45 + \frac{1}{2} \times 5 - 10 - 6 = 9.$$

Project 2

With the second project, the analogous calculation gives

$$a^* = \frac{3}{5} \text{ and } Eu_2(\frac{3}{5}) = \frac{3}{5} \times 48 - \frac{9}{5} \times 8 - 6 = 8.4.$$

However, the entrepreneur can only choose out of the set $\{0, \frac{1}{3}, \frac{1}{2}\}$. Given the concave shape of the maximand $(\frac{3}{5} > \frac{1}{2})$, we find

$$a_2^* = \frac{1}{2} \text{ and } Eu_2(\frac{1}{2}) = \frac{1}{2} \times 48 - 10 - 6 = 8.$$

Under both projects the level of effort chosen is $a = \frac{1}{2}$, but project C_1 yields a higher expected return, so the agent will prefer this project.

4.6.2 Debt-Financing

When D is the face value of debt, the entrepreneur has to pay back $\min\{D, C_i\}$.

Project 1

The entrepreneur solves (assuming $5 < D < 45$, which should trivially be true)

$$\max_a [a(45 - D) - 40a^2]$$

subject to the repayment (which will bind for the optimal solution)

$$aD + (1 - a)5 = 6.$$

Substituting in, we have

$$D = \frac{1 + 5a}{a}.$$

The problem now becomes

$$\max_a -1 + 40a - 40a^2$$

which eventually yields $a^* = \frac{1}{2}$. Thus, the optimal face value of debt is $D_1^* = 7$.

Project 2

With the alternative project, the maximization problem becomes

$$\max_a a(48 - D) - 40a^2$$

subject to

$$aD = 6.$$

Rewriting the problem we have

$$\max_a -6 + 48a - 40a^2$$

which yields $a^* = \frac{48}{80}$. Given the concavity of the problem we have $a = \frac{1}{2}$. Thus the optimal face value of debt is $D_1^* = 12$.

Unconditional Loan

If the loan is not conditional on the project chosen, then the entrepreneur will always end up choosing C_2 because

$$a(45 - D) < a(48 - D) \text{ for } \forall D.$$

In other words, the entrepreneur gets zero under both projects when cash flow is low. When cash flow is high, the residual is higher under project C_2. However, the investor will anticipate this choice. Therefore, if the entrepreneur cannot commit to a certain project, he will choose C_2 and get a debt contract consistent with this project ($D = 12$). Here the entrepreneur chooses $a = \frac{1}{2}$ since

$$\frac{1}{2}(48 - D) - \frac{40}{4} = 8 > \frac{1}{3}(48 - D) - \frac{40}{9} = 7.55$$

and the profit will be 8.

4.6.3 Equity-Financing

In case of the unconditional loan, the entrepreneur ends up with the dominated project 2. So she could potentially do better by issuing a share of equity s such that investors would get back the investment of 6 (in expectation). However, we need to check which effort levels such shares would induce to determine if the entrepreneur could indeed do better.

In the first project, the effort level $a = \frac{1}{2}$ will be chosen when

$$\frac{1}{2}50(1-s) - \frac{40}{4} > [\frac{1}{3}45 + \frac{2}{3}5](1-s) - \frac{40}{9}$$

which holds when $s < \frac{1}{6}$. Now to implement $a = \frac{1}{2}$ we need

$$s\left(\frac{1}{2} \times 45 + \frac{1}{2} \times 5\right) = 6.$$

However this induces $s = \frac{6}{25} > \frac{1}{6}$ so $a = \frac{1}{2}$ cannot be implemented.

For $a = \frac{1}{3}$ we need

$$s\left(\frac{1}{3} \times 45 + \frac{2}{3} \times 5\right) = 6.$$

This induces $s = \frac{18}{55} > \frac{1}{6}$ so $a = \frac{1}{3}$ can be implemented. However this yields a profit of

$$\frac{37}{55}(\frac{45}{3} + \frac{10}{3}) - \frac{40}{9} = 7.89 < 8$$

so debt is better.

Now looking at the second project, it is immediately clear that here debt and equity are the same, since neither have any payment in the low state. Thus the best that can be done is as above $a = \frac{1}{2}$ where the profits are 8.

Here the cutoff for choosing $a = \frac{1}{2}$ is

$$\frac{1}{2}48(1-s) - 40\frac{1}{4} > \frac{1}{3}48(1-s) - 40\frac{1}{9},$$

which holds when $s < \frac{11}{36}$. Now for $a = \frac{1}{2}$ we need

$$\frac{1}{2}48s = 6$$

or $s = \frac{1}{4} < \frac{11}{36}$. Hence, as expected $a = \frac{1}{2}$ is implementable and profits are

$$\frac{3}{4} \times \frac{1}{2} \times 48 - \frac{40}{4} = 8.$$

This is the same as under debt.

For $a = \frac{1}{3}$ we need

$$\frac{1}{3}48s = 6$$

or $s = \frac{18}{48} > \frac{11}{36}$. However, profits are

$$\frac{30}{48} \times \frac{1}{3} \times 48 - \frac{40}{9} = 5.55$$

and thus lower than for $a = \frac{1}{2}$.

So we get the same result as with debt and therefore cannot do better.

4.7 Question 16

Consider a target firm with widely dispersed ownership (atomistic risk-neutral shareholders) facing a takeover bid from a risk-neutral "raider." The monetary value per share under incumbent management is normalized to zero. Once the raider has gained control, she obtains a private benefit $Z \geq 0$ and can also exert effort a at private cost $ka^2/2$, which generates a value per share of aV_R where $V_R > k$.

Gaining control requires acquiring 50% of the shares of the target (the security voting structure is "one share, one vote"). Assume the raider does not own any shares prior to making the offer. There are no costs to the takeover other than the price the raider has to pay. Incumbent management is assumed to remain passive.

The raider makes a public tender offer of a price per share of b. This offer is "unrestricted" and "conditional"; that is, the raider buys all the shares tendered provided at least 50% of the shares of the firm are tendered. Faced with this offer, target shareholders noncooperatively choose whether to tender or not (assume that they think their tendering decision will not affect the outcome of the takeover).

1. Derive the posttakeover value per share, given that the raider has gained control and holds a fraction of shares $s \geq 50\%$.

2. At what bid price b will the raider be able to acquire a fraction of shares $s \geq 50\%$?

3. Derive the raider's optimal offer b^* and optimal posttakeover ownership stake s^*, respectively, when $Z = 0$ and $Z > 0$.

4. Is the raider's optimal bid efficient, that is, does it maximize the sum of shareholder and raider returns?

4.7.1 Posttakeover Value

Once the raider has gained control, holding a fraction of shares $s \geq 50\%$, she chooses an effort level that solves

$$\max_{a} saV_R - \frac{ka^2}{2}.$$

Hence, $a^*(s) = \frac{sV_R}{k}$ and the posttakeover value per share equals $a^*(s)V_R = \frac{sV_R^2}{k}$.

4.7.2   Bid Price

Every shareholder compares the bid of the raider with the expected posttakeover value of a share. Anticipating the optimal choice of effort $a^*(s)$ by the raider, the shareholder compares $\frac{sV_R^2}{k}$ to b. Therefore, whenever $b \geq \frac{sV_R^2}{k}$, all the shareholders are willing to sell their shares. Hence, by offering $b = \frac{sV_R^2}{k}$, the raider can obtain any fraction of shares $s \geq 50\%$ at the lowest price possible.

4.7.3   Second Best Contract

In order to determine whether she will place a takeover bid, the raider compares Z with

$$\max_{a,s,b} saV_R - sb - \frac{ka^2}{2}$$

subject to

$$0.5 \;\; \leq \;\; s \leq 1$$
$$a \;\; \in \;\; \arg\max_{a'} sa'V_R - \frac{ka'^2}{2}$$
$$b \;\; \geq \;\; aV_R.$$

We know that the incentive compatibility constraint can be replaced by $a^*(s) = \frac{sV_R}{k}$ and that the last constraint will be binding. Thus, the problem reduces to

$$\max_{a,s,b} -\frac{s^2V_R^2}{2k}$$

subject to

$$0.5 \leq s \leq 1.$$

Given that the value of the bids will exactly equal the posttakeover value of the shares, the principal will try to reduce the cost of efforts, constrained by $s \geq 50\%$. So in the second best optimum

$$s^* \;\; = \;\; \frac{1}{2}$$
$$a^* \;\; = \;\; \frac{V_R}{2k}$$
$$b^* \;\; = \;\; \frac{V_R^2}{2k}$$

However, the raider will place this bid only if

$$Z \geq \frac{V_R^2}{8k}.$$

If $Z = 0$, the raider will not try to take over the firm.

4.7.4   First Best Contract

The first best contract solves

$$\max_a aV_R - \frac{ka^2}{2}.$$

So in the first best optimum, we have

$$a^* = \frac{V_R}{k}.$$

Notice that the optimal effort level of the raider is higher in the first best optimum, but would be the same if the raider were to take over the entire firm.

Chapter 5

Disclosure of Private Information

5.1 Question 17

Consider a seller of a single item facing two buyers. The item is either worth v_H or $v_L < v_H$ (the buyers agree on these valuations; that is, it is a "common-value environment," as defined in Chapter 7) and the common prior probability is $\Pr(v = v_H) = 0.5$.

Suppose that the seller privately receives an estimate of the value of the item from an expert (in the form of a signed written letter) prior to the sale. There are n possible estimates e_i, with $i = 1, \ldots, n$. Assume $E[v \mid e_i] = v_i$ such that

$$v_1 < v_2 < \cdots < v_n$$

The buyers have no information about what the estimate is likely to be. Their beliefs are

$$\Pr(e_i) = \frac{1}{n}$$

1. Show that the unique equilibrium of the game where the seller sells the object through an ascending-price auction (or "English auction"; see Chapter 7) is for the seller to first disclose the content of the expert's estimate to the bidders.

2. What is the equilibrium in the English auction when the seller must pay a cost $K > 0$ to obtain an expert's assessment?

5.2 Question 18

Consider the following stylized example of trading by two risk-neutral market makers, each of them small enough that the *direct* influence of their trade on the stock prices is negligible. It is common knowledge that one of the traders will become informed about the true underlying value of a stock with probability β, while the other always remains uninformed. Assume each market maker can trade up to one unit twice in succession. The question is, should the market makers be required to disclose their first trade before they initiate their second trade? The question is considered at an ex ante stage where both market markers are identical and neither knows who will become informed (if any). So, at stage 0, the market makers must decide whether to introduce mandatory disclosure of trades at stage 1.

Prior to stage 1, the stock is worth either 110 or 90, with equal probabilities, so that the stock price is 100. At the beginning of stage 1, one market maker becomes informed about the value of the stock with probability β, while the other remains uninformed.

For the first trade, assume the uninformed market maker buys with probability 0.5 and sells with probability 0.5. Following the first trade, there may be mandatory or voluntary disclosure. Then a second trade can be initiated by both informed and uninformed market makers.

1. What are the ex post payoffs of the informed and uninformed traders under mandatory disclosure and no mandatory disclosure, respectively?

2. When is mandatory disclosure better from an ex ante perspective than no mandatory disclosure?

3. When there is no mandatory disclosure, when is there voluntary disclosure? Discuss.

5.2.1   Ex-Post Payoffs

Mandatory Disclosure

The informed market maker can clearly make 10 on the first trade. For the second trade, we need to distinguish between the various potential behaviors of the uninformed player. Clearly, when the uninformed player behaves differently than the informed player (the Buy-Sell and Sell-Buy cases) no inference can be made from the trades and thus the price stays at 100. It is thus only in the cases in which both parties behave the same way (the Buy-Buy and Sell-Sell cases) that the market can update its price. In the Buy-Buy case the new price will be: $100+10\beta$ while in the Sell-Sell case the price will be $100-10\beta$. This is due to the fact that only in the case where one of the parties is informed (which happens with β probability) should an inference up or down be made. An analogous result follows using the standard Bayesian updating formula. Thus in the Buy-Sell or Sell-Buy cases the informed player will make 10 in the second stage as well (a total of 20). In the Sell-Sell and Buy-Buy cases the price will move upward or downward and thus the informed party can make $10 - 10\beta = 10(1 - \beta)$ for a total of $20 - 10\beta$.

The uninformed player does not make anything on the first trade, since his information is no better than the information in the market. However, in the second stage, the uninformed player also benefits from the mandatory disclosure. This is due to the fact that in the second stage, the uninformed trader has better information than the market, since he knows that he is not informed and that his first trade was random. Thus he can make the difference between the expected price given his information, and the price in the market. Given that he is not informed, the probability that the other player is informed, equals

$$\Pr(A^{\text{Informed}}|B^{\text{Uninformed}}) \quad = \quad \frac{\Pr(A^{\text{Informed}} \cap B^{\text{Uninformed}})}{\Pr(B^{\text{Uninformed}})}$$

$$= \quad \frac{\frac{\beta}{2}}{1 - \frac{\beta}{2}} = \frac{\beta}{2 - \beta}.$$

Thus, the uninformed party updates the price up or down by $\frac{\beta}{2-\beta}$ and makes the difference between this amount and the movement of the price in the market. Accordingly, in the Buy-Sell and Sell-Buy cases, he makes $\frac{10\beta}{2-\beta}$, while in the Buy-Buy, Sell-Sell cases he makes

$$10\beta - \frac{10\beta}{2 - \beta}.$$

No Mandatory Disclosure

In this case, it is clear that the informed player has nothing to gain from disclosing his trade and sharing his private information. Thus the market will know this and disregard any disclosure of information, due to it being uninformative. The informed player can therefore make the full $10 + 10 = 20$ from the two trades, while the uninformed party has no informational advantage over the market and thus makes 0.

5.2.2   Comparison of Disclosure Regimes

From an ex ante perspective each player has $\frac{\beta}{2}$ probability of becoming informed. Thus, taking into account the fact that all 4 cases (Buy-Buy, Buy-Sell, Sell-Buy, Sell-Sell) are equally likely, we obtain the following ex ante payoffs.

In the mandatory regime,

$$\frac{\beta}{2}(20 - 5\beta) + (1 - \frac{\beta}{2})5\beta = 15\beta - 5\beta^2$$

and in the non-mandatory regime,

$$\frac{\beta}{2}(20) + (1 - \frac{\beta}{2})0 = 10\beta$$

Thus since $\beta \in [0, 1]$, it is clear that

$$5\beta > 5\beta^2$$

and the ex-ante payoffs are always higher in the mandatory disclosure regime.

5.2.3   Voluntary Disclosure

As mentioned above, we will never have informative disclosure under the voluntary disclosure rule. Thus we find that mandatory disclosure benefits the informed party (at the expense of the uninformed public). This result comes from the uncertainty in the market regarding the market maker's motive for trading. However, even though the mandatory disclosure is profitable ex ante, we need it to induce revelation of the trade by the informed party.

5.3   Question 19

Consider a two-period model with no discounting. A risk-neutral entrepreneur has a project generating at $t = 1$ a random cash flow $\pi \in \{\pi_L, \pi_H\}$ with $\pi_H > \pi_L$ and $\beta \equiv \Pr[\pi = \pi_L]$. The project requires an investment I at $t = 0$ that is raised from a risk-neutral creditor in a competitive capital market. Suppose that at $t = 1$, the entrepreneur observes π, but the creditor can verify π only by incurring a monitoring cost K (assume that verification costs are small enough for financing to be viable). Let

$$\beta\pi_L + (1 - \beta)\pi_H > I + K$$

and $I > \pi_L > K$, and assume that repayments must be nonnegative.

1. Assume that only deterministic monitoring contracts are feasible. Derive an optimal financial contract. Explain why there is no unique optimal contract within this setting.

2. Show that random verification is optimal. Explain.

3. Focus again on deterministic contracts, and suppose now that the entrepreneur is risk averse while the creditor remains risk neutral. Identify the unique optimal contract. Explain.

5.3.1   Unique Optimal Contract

Applying the revelation principle we can reduce the set of relevant contracts to those where the entrepreneur truthfully reveals π. When there is no verification, the contract can only specify a repayment $r(\hat{\pi})$ based on the announcement. However when there is verification the contract can specify a repayment contingent on both the announced return $\hat{\pi}$ and the verified return π, $r(\hat{\pi}, \pi)$. Application of the revelation principle ensures that in practice the entrepreneur always announces $\hat{\pi} = \pi$. Regardless, the contract will specify a different repayment when $\hat{\pi} \neq \pi$ to ensure that the entrepreneur has a sufficient incentive to truthfully reveal π. However, since this repayment never occurs in equilibrium it is efficient to provide the maximum incentive by setting $r(\hat{\pi}, \pi) = \pi$ whenever $\hat{\pi} \neq \pi$. There is no benefit from reporting a false return if it will be subsequently verified for sure. Returns are always truthfully revealed so we will denote the repayment contingent on the return π and announced return $\hat{\pi}$ as simply $r(\pi)$. Let the binary choice variables i_L and i_H denote whether the contract specifies that a low or a high reported cash flow triggers monitoring.

The objective is to minimize the costs of monitoring subject to satisfying the financier's participation constraint and the entrepreneur's incentive constraints. The problem can be written as

$$\min_{i_L, i_H, r(\pi_L), r(\pi_H)} K\left(\beta i_L + (1 - \beta)i_H\right)$$

subject to the financier's participation constraint

$$r(\pi_H)(1 - \beta) + r(\pi_L)\beta = I + K\left(\beta i_L + (1 - \beta)i_H\right), \qquad \text{(IR)}$$

a set of incentive constraints

$$\begin{aligned} r\left(\pi_L\right) &\leq r\left(\pi_H\right) \text{ if } i_L = 1 \text{ and } i_H = 0 & \text{(IC1)} \\ r\left(\pi_H\right) &\leq r\left(\pi_L\right) \text{ if } i_H = 1 \text{ and } i_L = 0 & \text{(IC2)} \\ r\left(\pi_H\right) &= r\left(\pi_L\right) \text{ if } i_L = 0 = i_H & \text{(IC3)} \end{aligned}$$

and a set of limited liability constraints

$$\begin{aligned} 0 &\leq r\left(\pi_H\right) \leq \pi_H & \text{(LL1)} \\ 0 &\leq r\left(\pi_L\right) \leq \pi_L. & \text{(LL2)} \end{aligned}$$

First note that we need the repayment $r(\pi_H) > r(\pi_L)$ so that the financier's participation constraint can be met subject to LL1 and LL2. In other words, we need this to ensure that the financier receives enough repayments to cover his investment and monitoring costs without violating a wealth constraint. Second, note that there is no need to monitor when a cash flow of π_H is reported. Third, low cash flows must be monitored. Otherwise, the entrepreneur will always report a low cash flow and the financier's participation cannot be met since $I > \pi_L$. The optimal contract is therefore one that only monitors low reported cash flows and specifies repayments such that the financier's participation constraint is met. There is no unique optimal contract here since any combination of repayments $r(\pi_H) \in (0, \pi_H]$ and $r(\pi_L) \in (0, \pi_L]$ that satisfies

$$r(\pi_H)(1 - \beta) + r(\pi_L)\beta = I + \beta K,$$

is feasible and minimizes monitoring costs. Unless random verification is allowed, further reduction of monitoring costs is not possible.

The assumptions of only deterministic contracts and bilateral risk neutrality allow there to be multiple optimal contracts in this question. While the binary choice variable to monitor or not for a realization of cash flow means the objective function can only take four potential values $(I, I+K, I+\beta K, I+(1-\beta)K)$, only one combination of the two binary variables does not violate either the incentive constraint of the entrepreneur or the participation constraint of the financier. The repayments $r(\pi_H)$ and $r(\pi_L)$ are therefore independent of the objective function and must only satisfy the constraints.

5.3.2   Optimal Random Verification

We introduce two new variables $p_L, p_H \in [0,1]$ to denote the probabilities of verification if a low or high cash flow is reported. We again appeal to the revelation principle and specify the maximum possible penalty for lying about the cash flow, that is $r(\hat{\pi}, \pi) = \pi$ whenever $\hat{\pi} \neq \pi$. The problem now becomes

$$\min_{p_L, p_H, r(\pi_L), r(\pi_H)} K\left(\beta p_L + (1-\beta)p_H\right)$$

subject to the financier's participation constraint

$$r(\pi_H)(1-\beta) + r(\pi_L)\beta \geq I + K\left(\beta p_L + (1-\beta)p_H\right), \tag{IR}$$

the set of incentive constraints

$$(\pi_H - r(\pi_H)) \geq (1 - p_L)(\pi_H - r(\pi_L)) \tag{IC1}$$
$$(\pi_L - r(\pi_L)) \geq (1 - p_H)(\pi_L - r(\pi_H)), \tag{IC2}$$

and the set of limited wealth constraints

$$0 \leq r(\pi_H) \leq \pi_H \tag{LL1}$$
$$0 \leq r(\pi_L) \leq \pi_L. \tag{LL2}$$

First, note we must have the repayment $r(\pi_H) > \pi_L$ so that the financier's participation constraint can be met subject to (LL1) and (LL2). Second, notice that this implies that the optimal choice of p_H is 0 since given the previous note (IC2) will never be violated and the (IR) is also relaxed. The problem is now reduced to minimizing p_L subject to the constraints. Third note that increasing $r(\pi_L)$ helps relax both (IC1) and (IR) so it should take its maximum possible value π_L. Now we can see that both (IR) and (IC1) must bind since if not we could reduce p_L and either increase or decrease $r(\pi_H)$ until both constraints bind. Rearranging (IC1) and substituting in $r(\pi_L) = \pi_L$ we get:

$$r(\pi_H) = p_L(\pi_H - \pi_L) + \pi_L.$$

Now substituting into (IR) we obtain

$$(p_L(\pi_H - \pi_L) + \pi_L)(1 - \beta) + \pi_L\beta = I + K\beta p_L.$$

Simplifying this expression we find

$$p_L = \frac{I - \pi_L}{(1-\beta)(\pi_H - \pi_L) - K\beta}.$$

Substituting back in for $r(\pi_H)$ yields

$$r(\pi_H) = \frac{I - \pi_L}{(1-\beta)(\pi_H - \pi_L) - K\beta}(\pi_H - \pi_L) + \pi_L.$$

5.3.3 Optimal Contract with Risk Averse Entrepreneur

The setup is similar again to part 1 except that we now have a risk-averse entrepreneur. The optimal contract is therefore the one from amongst those found in the solution to part 1 which minimizes risk taken on by the entrepreneur. The expected value of the project is

$$\pi_H(1-\beta) + \pi_L\beta - (I + \beta K),$$

where $I + \beta K$ is the expected investment and monitoring cost. If it is feasible, the optimal contract is the one in which the entrepreneur receives the same expected payoff under both a high and a low cash flow. Otherwise the optimal contract is the one in which the difference between the entrepreneur's payoff under the two scenarios is minimized.

If $K \geq \frac{(1-\beta)(\pi_H - \pi_L) - I}{\beta}$ then we can have $\pi_H - r(\pi_H) = \pi_L - r(\pi_L) > 0$ (with an expected repayment of $I + \beta K$) where:

$$
\begin{aligned}
r(\pi_H) &= I + \beta K + \beta(\pi_H - \pi_L) \\
r(\pi_L) &= I + \beta K - (1-\beta)(\pi_H - \pi_L)
\end{aligned}
$$

Otherwise if $K < \frac{(1-\beta)(\pi_H - \pi_L) - I}{\beta}$,

$$
\begin{aligned}
r(\pi_H) &= \frac{I + \beta K}{1 - \beta} \\
r(\pi_L) &= 0.
\end{aligned}
$$

5.4 Question 20

Consider a financial contracting problem between a wealth-constrained, risk-neutral entrepreneur and a wealthy risk-neutral investor. The cost of investment at date $t = 0$ is I. The project generates a random return on investment at date $t = 1$ of $\pi(\theta, I) = 2\min\{\theta, I\}$, where θ is the state of nature, uniformly distributed on $[0, 1]$.

1. Characterize the first-best level of investment, I^{FB}.

2. Suppose that the realized return at $t = 1$ is freely observable only to the entrepreneur. A cost $K > 0$ must be paid for the investor to observe $\pi(\theta, I)$. Derive the second-best contract under the assumptions of (a) deterministic verification and (b) zero expected profit for the investor, taking into account that repayments cannot exceed realized returns (net of inspection costs).

3. Show that the second-best optimal investment level is lower than I^{FB}.

Chapter 6

Multidimensional Incentive Problems

6.1 Question 21

A risk-neutral profit-maximizing monopolist producing two goods, good 1 and good 2, faces a consumer with utility function $v_1 q_1 + v_2 q_2 - T$ where T is the payment from the consumer to the monopolist, q_i is the quantity of good i ($i = 1, 2$) bought by the consumer, and v_i is the consumer's valuation for good i. The monopolist's cost is $c(q_1) + c(q_2)$. Each consumer valuation v_i can take two values, v_i^L and v_i^H. Define $\Delta v_i \equiv v_i^H - v_i^L > 0$. Assume that v_1 and v_2 are independently distributed and $\Pr(v_i = v_i^L) = \beta_i$. The monopolist does not observe the realization of the v_i's, but their distribution is common knowledge.

1. Suppose that the monopolist decides to treat the contract-design problem as two separate problems, one for each good. What is the second-best outcome?

2. Assume that the monopolist now decides to consider a general contract instead of two separate ones. How many (IC) constraints does the monopolist face? How many (IR) constraints? (Do not write them down.)

3. Consider the relaxed problem with only the following constraints: (a) the (IR) constraint for type (v_1^L, v_2^L); and (b) the following four (IC) constraints: for type (v_1^H, v_2^L) versus type (v_1^L, v_2^L), (IC1); for type (v_1^L, v_2^H) versus type (v_1^L, v_2^L), (IC2); for type (v_1^H, v_2^H) versus type (v_1^H, v_2^L), (IC3); and for type (v_1^H, v_2^H) versus type (v_1^L, v_2^H), (IC4). Write down this relaxed problem.

4. Show that for this relaxed problem the (IR) constraint for (v_1^L, v_2^L) is binding. Show that constraints (IC1) and (IC2) are also binding. Use these results to eliminate from the monopolist's problem the payments

it gets from types (v_1^L, v_2^L), (v_1^H, v_2^L), and (v_1^L, v_2^H). That is, write the relaxed problem as a maximization problem with respect to quantities and the payment the monopolist gets from type (v_1^H, v_2^H), subject to the two constraints (IC3) and (IC4).

5. Write the Lagrangian of this last problem. Denote by λ_1 and λ_2 the Lagrange multipliers of (IC3) and (IC4), respectively. Show that $\lambda_1 + \lambda_2 = 1/\left[(1 - \beta_1)(1 - \beta_2)\right]$. Show that the quantities of good i ($i = 1, 2$) sold to the types who have a high valuation for that good are as in part 1 of this question. Discuss.

6. Write down the first-order conditions for the quantities of good i ($i = 1, 2$) sold to the types who have a low valuation for that good. Show that λ_1 and λ_2 are strictly positive. Compare them to the answer of part 1. Discuss.

7. Consider the symmetric case $v_1^L = v_2^L = v^L$, $v_1^H = v_2^H = v^H$, $\beta_1 = \beta_2 = \beta$. Show that the solution to the relaxed problem is also the solution to the initial problem.

6.2   Question 22

Consider an agent who works for a risk-neutral principal. The agent can allocate time to $n + 1$ tasks. Call a_i the amount of time spent on task i ($i = 0, 1, 2, ..., n$). The principal cares only about task 0, getting output $q = a_0 + \varepsilon$, where ε is normally distributed with mean 0 and with variance σ^2. The agent, however, derives a benefit $v_i(a_i)$ from spending time on tasks $i = 1, 2, ..., n$. She has CARA risk preferences, and her utility function is

$$-e^{-\eta[w - \psi(a_0 + a_1 + ... + a_n) + v_1(a_1) + v_2(a_2) + ... + v_n(a_n)]}$$

where $\psi(a_0 + a_1 + ... + a_n)$ is the cost of time, with ψ' and $\psi'' > 0$ and $\psi(0) = 0$. Assume also that $v_i' > 0$, $v_i'' < 0$, and $v_i(0) = 0$, and that optimization with respect to the a_i's leads to interior solutions. Call w_0 the agent's reservation wage.

1. Derive the first-best outcome. Discuss.

2. Assume that the principal does not observe the a_i's chosen by the agent, but only q and whether the agent can engage at all in any of the tasks $1, 2, ..., n$. Assume the principal can offer the agent a linear incentive scheme $t + sq$ and he can also choose the subset S of tasks the agent is allowed to engage in (that is, for any other task j, the principal can force $a_j = 0$). Determine the optimal subset S as a function of s. What happens when $s = 1$? Compare with the answer in part 1 of this question. What happens when s drops below 1? Discuss.

6.2.1 First-Best Outcome

This question is based on Holmstrom & Milgrom (1991). The principal can observe and contract on actions and maximizes

$$E\pi = a_0 - Ew.$$

With normally distributed noise and exponential utility we can rewrite the agent's certainty equivalent as

$$Eu = Ew - \frac{\eta}{2}\text{var}(w) - \psi\left(a_0 + \sum_{i=1}^{n} a_i\right) + \sum_{i=1}^{n} v_i(a_i).$$

Hence, the first-best solution solves

$$\max_{a_0, a_i, w(a)} E\pi = a_0 - Ew(a)$$

subject to

$$Ew(a) - \frac{\eta}{2}\text{var}(w(a)) - \psi\left(a_0 + \sum_{i=1}^{n} a_i\right) + \sum_{i=1}^{n} v_i(a_i) \geq w_0$$

This yields the first order conditions

$$1 = \psi'\left(a_0^* + \sum_{i=1}^{n} a_i^*\right)$$

$$v_i'(a_i^*) = \psi'\left(a_0^* + \sum_{i=1}^{n} a_i^*\right),$$

so that for all $i = 1, 2, ..., n$ we have

$$v_i'(a_i^*) = 1.$$

Finally, the wage received by the agent is constant and is given by

$$w = w_0 + \psi\left(a_o^* + \sum_{i=1}^{n} a_i^*\right) - \sum_{i=1}^{n} v_i(a_i^*).$$

6.2.2 Linear Contracts

The principal's problem is to solve

$$\max_{a,t,s} a_0 - t - sa_0$$

subject to

$$t + sa_0 - \frac{\eta}{2}s^2\sigma^2 - \psi\left(a_0 + \sum_{i \in S} a_i\right) + \sum_{i \in S} v_i(a_i) \geq w_0 \qquad \text{(IR)}$$

and

$$a \in \arg\max t + sa_0 - \frac{\eta}{2}s^2\sigma^2 - \psi\left(a_0 + \sum_{i \in S} a_i\right) + \sum_{i \in S} v_i(a_i) \qquad \text{(IC)}$$

where $S \subset I = \{0, 1, 2, ..., n\}$.

The agent's first order conditions for a_0 and a_i yield

$$s = \psi'\left(a_0 + \sum_{i \in S} a_i\right)$$

$$v_i'(a_i) = \psi'\left(a_0 + \sum_{i \in S} a_i\right).$$

Hence, for all $i = 1, 2, ..., n$ we have

$$v_i'(a_i) = s,$$

so that the time spent on task i given by $a_i(s)$ depends only on s and not on S. Furthermore, the total time spent working $a_0 + \sum_{i \in S} a_i$ is independent of S and also only depends on s.

For a given s, we can now determine the optimal $S(s)$. Using (IR) and (IC), the principal's expected profit is

$$E\pi = a_0 - \frac{\eta}{2}s^2\sigma^2 - \psi\left(a_0 + \sum_{i \in S} a_i\right) + \sum_{i \in S} v_i(a_i) - w_0.$$

The benefit the principal gets from allowing the agent to allocate time to task i is $v_i(a_i(s))$, while the opportunity cost is the time the agent reallocates from task 0 to task i which is given by a_i. Furthermore, for a given s, the increase in marginal cost from the additional time allocated to task i must be counterbalanced by a decrease in the time allocated to activity 0. The optimal set of allowable tasks therefore is

$$S(s) = \{i \in I | v_i(a_i(s)) - a_i(s) > 0\}.$$

From the first order conditions we can see that when $s = 1$ the first-best actions will be chosen. However, the base rate t now includes a risk premium

$$t = w_o - a_0 - \frac{\eta}{2}s^2\sigma^2 + \psi\left(a_o + \sum_{i \in S} v_i(a_i)\right) - \sum_{i \in S} v_i(a_i).$$

More importantly, the optimal set of allowable tasks when $s = 1$ includes all tasks, that is $S(s = 1) = I$ which again follows from $v_i'(a_i) = s = 1$ and $v_i(a_i(1)) > a_i(1)$. Hence, when $s = 1$ we have the same answer as in part 1.

Since v_i is strictly concave, $a_i(s)$ is decreasing in s. Hence, when s drops below 1, the time allocated to tasks with private benefits will rise. Furthermore, the optimal set of allowable tasks S will shrink. To see this, rewrite the condition for the optimal set of allowable tasks as

$$S(s) = \{i \in I | \frac{v_i(a_i(s))}{a_i(s)} > 1\}.$$

As s decreases both $v_i(a_i(s))$ and $a_i(s)$ increase, but since v_i is concave in a_i, the fraction $\frac{v_i(a_i(s))}{a_i(s)}$ will eventually fall below 1 and the task i will no longer be included in S.

6.3 Question 23

Consider a risk-neutral principal who has to take a decision $\in \{A, 0, B\}$. The optimal decision depends on a random parameter $\theta = \theta_A + \theta_B$. Ex ante, we have $\Pr(\theta_A = -1) = \beta = \Pr(\theta_B = 1)$ and $\Pr(\theta_A = 0) = 1 - \beta = \Pr(\theta_B = 0)$. Moreover, θ_A and θ_B are independently distributed. Assume that the optimal decision is A if $\theta = -1$, 0 if $\theta = 0$, and B if $\theta = 1$. Let K be the cost to the principal of not taking the optimal decision for any θ.

The principal has access to a population of risk-neutral agents who, by spending one unit of effort looking at θ_i ($i = A, B$), can obtain hard evidence that $|\theta_i| = 1$. Specifically, if $\theta_i = 0$, no evidence is found, while if $|\theta_i| = 1$, hard evidence (that is, evidence that cannot be forged) is found with probability p. Agents' utility functions are $w - n\psi$, where w is their wage, n the number of units of effort expended by the agent ($n = 2$ means that the agent looks at both θ_A and θ_B), and ψ the unit cost of effort.

1. What is the first best-effort level in this case? When is it optimal to have two units of effort expended?

2. Assume that agents privately choose effort but can be paid per piece of evidence provided. Can the first-best effort level be achieved while leaving no rents to the agent(s)? Does it matter whether one or two agents (expending, respectively, two or one units of effort) are hired by the principal? Does the outcome depend on agents' limited-liability constraint $w \geq 0$?

3. Assume now that the hard evidence is automatically transmitted to the principal but that contracts can be contingent only on the *decision* taken by the principal, and not on the amount of information generated by the agent(s). What is the optimal contract for the principal [i.e., the contract that minimizes the expected cost of wrong decisions plus the wage bill to be conceded to the agent(s)] when a single agent is hired by the principal? And when two agents are hired by the principal? Does this depend on agents' limited-liability constraints?

4. Assume finally that, whenever the hard evidence is generated, it is first obtained by the agent, who can then decide whether or not to disclose it to the principal. Does this new sequence of moves change the conclusion reached in part 3 of this question?

6.3.1   First-Best Solution

We compare the conditions for which exerting no effort, one unit of effort or two units of efforts is optimal. In order to know the expected cost, we first need to find the optimal decision rule based on the found evidence. Define $C(n)$ as the sum of the expected cost from the potential of making the wrong decision, using the optimal decision rule, and the actual cost from exerting n unit(s) of effort. Here the problem is to find n that minimizes this loss, that is n^* is defined by

$$n^* = \arg\min_{n \in \{0,1,2\}} C(n).$$

For notational simplicity I write that $\theta_i = \emptyset$ when effort was exerted to find evidence on i, but no evidence was found.

No Effort $(n = 0)$

In the absence of any effort being exerted, we know that

$$
\begin{aligned}
\Pr(\theta &= 1) = \beta(1-\beta) \\
\Pr(\theta &= 0) = \beta^2 + (1-\beta)^2 \\
\Pr(\theta &= 1) = (1-\beta)\beta.
\end{aligned}
$$

Now it is clear that $d = 0$. To see this, compare the expected loss from choosing $d = 0$ and $d = i$. The condition for $d = 0$ to be optimal is

$$\left[1 - \beta^2 + (1-\beta)^2\right] K < \left[1 - \beta(1-\beta)\right] K$$

$\Leftrightarrow$

$$\beta(1-\beta) < \frac{1}{3}.$$

The above condition is always satisfied, so $d = 0$ is always optimal. Hence, the expected cost equals

$$
\begin{aligned}
C(0) &= [1 - (\beta^2 + (1-\beta)^2)]K \\
&= 2\beta(1-\beta)K.
\end{aligned}
$$

One Unit of Effort $(n = 1)$

Since the cases for exerting effort on finding evidence for A and B are symmetric, we concentrate on A.

When one unit of effort is exerted, evidence is found $(\theta_A = -1)$ with probability $p\beta$ and the posterior probabilities are

$$
\begin{aligned}
\Pr(\theta &= -1|\theta_A = -1) = 1 - \beta \\
\Pr(\theta &= 0|\theta_A = -1) = \beta \\
\Pr(\theta &= 1|\theta_A = -1) = 0.
\end{aligned}
$$

It is optimal to choose $d = A$ when

$$1 - \beta > \beta$$

$\Leftrightarrow$

$$\beta < \frac{1}{2}.$$

Otherwise it is optimal to choose $d = 0$.

When one unit of effort is exerted, no evidence is found (that is $\theta_A = \emptyset$) with probability $1 - p\beta$. Using Bayes' rule we find that the posterior probability is given by

$$\Pr(\theta_A = -1 | \theta_A = \emptyset) = \frac{\beta(1 - p)}{\beta(1 - p) + (1 - \beta)} = \frac{(1 - p)\beta}{1 - p\beta} \equiv \hat{\beta} \leq \beta.$$

The posterior probabilities are

$$\begin{aligned}
\Pr(\theta &= -1 | \theta_A = \emptyset) = \hat{\beta}(1 - \beta) \\
\Pr(\theta &= 0 | \theta_A = \emptyset) = \hat{\beta}\beta + (1 - \hat{\beta})(1 - \beta) \\
\Pr(\theta &= 1 | \theta_A = \emptyset) = (1 - \hat{\beta})\beta.
\end{aligned}$$

Notice that $d = A$ is dominated by the other two decisions since $\hat{\beta} \leq \beta$. Hence, the decision is between $d = B$ and $d = 0$. It is optimal to choose $d = 0$ when

$$\hat{\beta}\beta + (1 - \hat{\beta})(1 - \beta) > (1 - \hat{\beta})\beta$$

$\Leftrightarrow$

$$\frac{(1 - \beta)\beta}{1 - p\beta} < \frac{1}{3}.$$

Thus the expected cost when using one unit of effort is the cost of employing the best possible decision

$$C(1) = \psi + p\beta \min\{\beta, 1 - \beta\}K$$
$$+ (1 - p\beta)\min\{1 - \hat{\beta}\beta - (1 - \hat{\beta})(1 - \beta), 1 - (1 - \hat{\beta})\beta\}K$$

$\Leftrightarrow$

$$C(1) = \psi + p\beta \min\{\beta, 1 - \beta\}K$$
$$+ (1 - p\beta)\left[1 - \frac{1}{1 - p\beta}\max\{(1 - p)\beta^2 + (1 - \beta)^2, (1 - \beta)\beta\}\right]K$$

Two Units of Effort $(n = 2)$

Finally, when 2 units of effort are exerted we have 4 options, of which the first 2 are symmetric:

1. Evidence is found for A but not for B. This happens with probability

$$
\begin{aligned}
\Pr(\theta_A &= -1, \theta_B = \emptyset) = p\beta[(1 - \beta) + \beta(1 - p)] \\
&= p\beta(1 - p\beta).
\end{aligned}
$$

The associated posterior probabilities are

$$
\begin{aligned}
\Pr(\theta &= -1|\theta_A = -1, \theta_B = \emptyset) = 1 - \hat{\beta} \\
\Pr(\theta &= 0|\theta_A = -1, \theta_B = \emptyset) = \hat{\beta} \\
\Pr(\theta &= 1|\theta_A = -1, \theta_B = \emptyset) = 0.
\end{aligned}
$$

Thus, $d = A$ is optimal if and only if

$$
\hat{\beta} < \frac{1}{2}.
$$

2. Evidence is found for B but not for A. As before,

$$
\Pr(\theta_A = \emptyset, \theta_B = -1) = p\beta(1 - p\beta)
$$

and

$$
\begin{aligned}
\Pr(\theta &= -1|\theta_A = -1, \theta_B = \emptyset) = 0 \\
\Pr(\theta &= 0|\theta_A = -1, \theta_B = \emptyset) = \hat{\beta} \\
\Pr(\theta &= 1|\theta_A = -1, \theta_B = \emptyset) = 1 - \hat{\beta}.
\end{aligned}
$$

Choosing $d = B$ is optimal if and only if

$$
\hat{\beta} < \frac{1}{2}.
$$

3. No evidence is found. This happens with probability

$$
\begin{aligned}
\Pr(\theta_A &= \emptyset, \theta_B = \emptyset) = [(1 - \beta) + \beta(1 - p)]^2 \\
&= (1 - p\beta)^2.
\end{aligned}
$$

The posteriors are

$$
\begin{aligned}
\Pr(\theta &= -1|\theta_A = \emptyset, \theta_B = \emptyset) = \hat{\beta}(1 - \hat{\beta}) \\
\Pr(\theta &= 0|\theta_A = \emptyset, \theta_B = \emptyset) = \hat{\beta}^2 + (1 - \hat{\beta})^2 \\
\Pr(\theta &= 1|\theta_A = \emptyset, \theta_B = \emptyset) = (1 - \hat{\beta})\hat{\beta}
\end{aligned}
$$

In this case it is always optimal to choose $d = 0$ since the condition

$$
\hat{\beta}(1 - \hat{\beta}) < \frac{1}{3}
$$

is always satisfied.

4. Evidence is found for both. This happens with probability:

$$\Pr(\theta_A = -1, \theta_B = 1) = p^2\beta^2.$$

The posteriors are

$$\Pr(\theta = -1|\theta_A = -1, \theta_B = 1) = 0$$
$$\Pr(\theta = 0|\theta_A = -1, \theta_B = 1) = 1$$
$$\Pr(\theta = 1|\theta_A = -1, \theta_B = 1) = 0.$$

In this case, clearly $d = 0$ is optimal and the right decision is always taken.

As a result of these four cases, the expected cost when 2 units of effort are used is

$$C(2) = 2\psi + 2p\beta(1 - p\beta)\min\{\hat{\beta}, 1 - \hat{\beta}\}K + (1 - p\beta)^2\left[1 - \hat{\beta}^2 - (1 - \hat{\beta})^2\right]K$$
$$= 2\psi + 2p\beta\min\{(1 - p)\beta, 1 - \beta\}K + 2(1 - p)\beta(1 - \beta)K.$$

Comparison

In the first best the number of effort units with the lowest expected cost will be chosen. That is, we need to compare $C(0)$, $C(1)$, and $C(2)$. These expressions contain minimum and maximum terms. The three pairs are

$$\{\beta, 1 - \beta\}, \{(1 - \beta)\beta, (1 - p)\beta^2 + (1 - \beta)^2\} \text{ and } \{(1 - p)\beta, 1 - \beta\}$$

so there are many potential cases to check. First, note though that when $\beta < 1 - \beta$, this implies

$$(1 - p)\beta < 1 - \beta$$

and

$$(1 - \beta)\beta < (1 - p)\beta^2 + (1 - \beta)^2.$$

Moreover, when $\beta > 1 - \beta$, then $(1 - \beta)\beta > (1 - p)\beta^2 + (1 - \beta)^2$ implies that

$$(1 - p)\beta < 1 - \beta.$$

This leaves us with 4 cases for which we have to compute $C(n)$.

1. $\{\beta < 1 - \beta\}$
   The expected costs are

$$C(0) = 2\beta(1 - \beta)K$$
$$C(1) = 2\beta(1 - \beta)K - p\beta(1 - 2\beta)K + \psi$$
$$C(2) = 2\beta(1 - \beta)K - 2p\beta(1 - 2\beta)K - 2p^2\beta^2K + 2\psi.$$

Comparing these expressions, we first notice that $\min\{C(0), C(2)\} < C(1)$ so that one unit of effort is never optimal. If

$$\psi \le p\beta\left[1 - \beta(2 - p)\right]K,$$

then $C(2) < C(1)$. If

$$\psi > p\beta \left[1 - \beta(2 - p)\right] K,$$

then $C(0) < C(1)$. Hence, $n = 2$ is optimal if and only if

$$\psi < p\beta(1 - 2\beta)K + p^2\beta^2 K.$$

Otherwise, $n = 0$ is optimal.

2. $\{\beta > 1 - \beta\}, \{(1 - \beta)\beta > (1 - p)\beta^2 + (1 - \beta)^2\}$
   The expected costs are

$$
\begin{aligned}
C(0) &= 2\beta(1 - \beta)K \\
C(1) &= 2\beta(1 - \beta)K - \left[3\beta(1 - \beta) + p\beta^2 - 1\right]K + \psi \\
C(2) &= 2\beta(1 - \beta)K - 2p\beta\left[1 - \beta(2 - p)\right]K + 2\psi.
\end{aligned}
$$

Again, $n = 2$ is optimal if and only if

$$\psi < p\beta\left[1 - \beta(2 - p)\right]K$$

and $n = 0$ is optimal otherwise.

3. $\{\beta > 1 - \beta\}, \{(1 - \beta)\beta < (1 - p)\beta^2 + (1 - \beta)^2\}, \{(1 - p)\beta < 1 - \beta\}$
   The expected costs are

$$
\begin{aligned}
C(0) &= 2\beta(1 - \beta)K \\
C(1) &= 2\beta(1 - \beta)K + \psi \\
C(2) &= 2\beta(1 - \beta)K - 2p\beta\left[1 - \beta(2 - p)\right]K + 2\psi.
\end{aligned}
$$

Clearly, $C(0) < C(1)$, so we only need to compare $n = 0$ and $n = 2$. As before, $n = 2$ is optimal if and only if

$$\psi < p\beta\left[1 - \beta(2 - p)\right]K$$

and $n = 0$ is optimal otherwise.

4. $\{\beta > 1 - \beta\}, \{(1 - \beta)\beta < (1 - p)\beta^2 + (1 - \beta)^2\}, \{(1 - p)\beta > 1 - \beta\}$
   The expected costs are

$$
\begin{aligned}
C(0) &= 2\beta(1 - \beta)K \\
C(1) &= 2\beta(1 - \beta)K + \psi \\
C(2) &= 2\beta(1 - \beta)K + 2\psi
\end{aligned}
$$

so here it is optimal to choose $n = 0$.

From the analysis, it is clear that it is never optimal to set $n = 1$ and the decision is only between $n = 2$ and $n = 0$. Note, that in case 4 the optimal decision is always $n = 0$. However, we can rule out this case if we assume that

$\hat{\beta} < \frac{1}{2}$ as Dewatripont & Tirole (1999) do in their analysis. This assumption is equivalent to saying that if evidence was found for i, but no evidence was found for $-i$ (that is, $|\theta_i| = 1, \theta_{-i} = \emptyset$), it is better to choose $d = i$ rather than $d = 0$. To summarize, for case 1 we get

$$n^* = \begin{cases} 0 \text{ if } \psi \geq p\beta(1 - 2\beta)K + p^2\beta^2 K \\ 2 \text{ if } \psi < p\beta(1 - 2\beta)K + p^2\beta^2 K \end{cases},$$

and for cases 2 and 3 we get

$$n^* = \begin{cases} 0 \text{ if } \psi \geq p\beta \left[1 - \beta(2 - p)\right] K \\ 2 \text{ if } \psi < p\beta \left[1 - \beta(2 - p)\right] K \end{cases},$$

and for case 4 we get

$$n^* = 0.$$

In other words, only if the cost of search effort is sufficiently low, it may be optimal to have two units of effort expended. In what follows we assume that $\hat{\beta} < \frac{1}{2}$ so that the above conditions are the only determinant of whether 0 or 2 units of effort are optimal.

6.3.2 Evidence-Based Rewards

From the previous section we know that it is never optimal in the first best to have $n = 1$. Let w_{AB}, w_i and w_0 denote the wages when evidence is found for A and B, for A or B and when no evidence is found respectively. For simplicity, for this section set $w_0 = 0$ and $w_i = w$. Obviously, if the optimal effort is $n = 0$ then we can just set $w_{AB} = w_i = w_0 = 0$, so the agent will exert no effort.

Single Agent

If the optimal effort is $n = 2$ then incentive compatibility requires that the agent prefers investigating both causes to one or none,

$$p^2\beta^2 w_{AB} + 2p\beta(1 - p\beta)w - 2\psi \geq p\beta w_i - \psi$$
$$p^2\beta^2 w_{AB} + 2p\beta(1 - p\beta)w - 2\psi \geq 0.$$

One of the incentive compatible efficient contracts is

$$w = w_0 = 0$$
$$w_{AB} = \frac{2\psi}{p^2\beta^2}.$$

With this contract the participation constraint will be binding and no rents are left to the agent. Limited liability restricts the set of feasible efficient contracts, but the set is still non-empty. For example, the above contract will work.

Advocates

In order to be incentive compatible, the contract needs to specify wages such that both agents prefer spending one unit of effort looking at θ_i to shirking given that the other agent does not shirk. That is when setting $w_0 = 0$ the agent's incentive compatibility constraint is

$$p\beta w - \psi \geq 0.$$

Clearly, the wage is

$$w = \frac{\psi}{p\beta}.$$

The efficient outcome will be attained in a dominant strategy equilibrium since one agent's action does not influence the other agent's payoff. Again, no rents are left to the agents and the limited liability constraint does not prevent us from attaining the first best. Note that the expected wages to be paid by the principal are the same in the single agent and advocates case respectively,

$$p^2\beta^2 w_{AB} = \beta pw + \beta pw = 2\psi.$$

Due to the linearity of the cost function, it makes no difference to the principal to use one or two agents to implement the efficient level of effort.

6.3.3   Decision-Based Rewards

Compared with the evidence-based rewards, the decision-based rewards imply one extra restriction, namely

$$w_{AB} = w_0.$$

If hard evidence is found for θ_A and θ_B, the principal will make the same decision $d = 0$ as when he has no evidence at all. At the optimum, we will also have $w_A = w_B = w$.

Single Agent

The probability of finding hard evidence for only θ_A or θ_B when looking at both equals

$$\Pr(|\theta_i| = 1, \theta_{-i} = \emptyset) = 2p\beta(1 - p\beta) = 2x(1 - x)$$

where $x = p\beta$. Incentive compatibility requires that the agent prefers investigating both to one or none, that is

$$x(1 - x)(w_A + w_B) + [1 - 2x(1 - x)]\,w_0 - 2\psi$$
$$\geq x \max\{w_A + w_B\} + (1 - x)w_0 - \psi$$

$$x(1 - x)(w_A + w_B) + [1 - 2x(1 - x)]\,w_0 - 2\psi \geq w_0.$$

These two conditions can be rewritten as

$$x(1 - 2x)[w - w_0] \geq \psi$$
$$x(1 - x)[w - w_0] \geq \psi,$$

where we noted that at the optimum $w_A = w_B = w$. Given that $x = p\beta < 1$, the second condition implies that w must be greater than w_0. Together with the first condition, this implies that the efficient effort level cannot be attained through an incentive compatible contract when $x = p\beta \geq \frac{1}{2}$. If $x < \frac{1}{2}$, the optimal contract inducing two units of effort requires

$$w - w_0 = \frac{\psi}{x(1 - 2x)}$$

and w_0 is set such that the agent receives no rent. In particular,

$$w_0 = -\frac{2x\psi}{1 - 2x} < 0.$$

This implements $n^* = 2$ without leaving rents to the agent, but it requires $x < \frac{1}{2}$ and $w_0 < 0$.

Clearly, if there is limited liability, the above contract is no longer feasible and instead it is optimal to set

$$w_0 = 0$$
$$w = \frac{\psi}{x(1 - 2x)},$$

but this leaves a rent to the agent which in this case of $n = 2$ is equal to

$$R(2) = 2x(1 - x)w - 2\psi = \frac{2\psi x}{1 - 2x}.$$

Thus the principal's problem is now given by

$$\min_n C(n) + R(n).$$

It may be that because of this rent the principal prefers to induce one unit of effort or no effort at all. The comparison between $n = 2$ and $n = 0$ is straightforward as $R(0) = 0$ and so the conditions only need to be modified to incorporate $R(2)$. However, $n = 1$ may now be optimal from the principal's point of view for some values of ψ since $R(1) = 0$ even under limited liability. To see this note that the (IC) constraint for $n = 1$ is

$$xw + (1 - x)w_0 - \psi \geq w_0.$$

The optimal contract (under limited liability) is

$$w_0 = 0 \text{ and } w_i = \frac{\psi}{\beta p}.$$

No rents are left to the agent, and thus indeed $R(1) = 0$. The limited liability constraint restricts the set of feasible efficient contracts, but the set is still non-empty. Thus, if the rents $R(2)$ from implementing $n = 2$ become too large, it may be better to implement the inefficient choice $n = 1$ or $n = 0$, which always leave no rents to the agent. However, as we will see, this is of no concern since the principal can always do better by hiring two agents rather than one agent.

Advocates

Given that the rewards can be based on the different decisions and two different agents are hired, the principal could introduce a different reward structure. For example, agent 1 is instructed to search for evidence on θ_i and is paid w when $d = i$ and w_0 when $d = \{0, -i\}$ and conversely for agent 2. Incentive compatibility requires that every agent prefers to exert the effort allocated given that the opponent does,

$$x(1 - x)w + [1 - x(1 - x)] w_0 - \psi \geq w_0.$$

The optimal contract implements the first best and is given by

$$\begin{aligned} w_0 &= 0 \\ w &= \frac{\psi}{x(1 - x)}. \end{aligned}$$

Clearly, the limited liability constraint is of no importance here. Further, note that in contrast with the single agent-case, the optimal solution is not restricted by $\beta p < \frac{1}{2}$. Moreover, the competition enables the principal to extract all rents from the agent, whereas to induce a single agent to exert the second unit of effort, she needs to offer a wage that leaves the agent rents if he exerts a single effort and is protected by limited liability. The advocates setting always dominates the single agent setting and allows us to implement the first best when $n = 2$ or when $n = 0$. As shown before, $n = 1$ is never optimal anyway. The reason is that only the aggregate performance which is non-monotonic in the effort expended in each task can be observed.

6.3.4   Information Disclosure

Whenever two agents are used, the decision-based rewards are monotonic in te success of the agent in finding hard evidence. Therefore, each agent has no incentive not to disclose the hard evidence he found and so our analysis of the advocates case is unaffected and the first best is still attainable.

However, when a single agent expends two units of efforts and finds hard evidence for θ_A and θ_B, he will never disclose both pieces of evidence with the contract specified in the previous section. When disclosing both, he would receive $w_0 = 0$ instead of $w = \frac{\psi}{x(1-x)}$.

Note first that the posteriors about θ_A and θ_B, given the disclosed evidence, are different now. Assuming that the optimal decision rule is still $d = i$ when

$|\theta_i| = 1$ and $|\theta_{-i}| = 0$, which requires $\hat{\beta} < \frac{1}{2}$ as discussed before, and $d = 0$ when $|\theta_i| = |\theta_{-i}|$, the expected cost of inducing two levels of effort is changed. Assuming that the new condition for $n^* = 2$ holds, the incentive compatibility constraints become

$$x(2-x)w + [1 - x(2-x)]\,w_0 - 2\psi \ \geq \ xw + (1-x)w_0 - \psi$$
$$x(2-x)w + [1 - x(2-x)]\,w_0 - 2\psi \ \geq \ w_0.$$

This can be rewritten as

$$x(1-x)[w - w_0] \ \geq \ \psi$$
$$x(1 - \frac{x}{2})[w - w_0] \ \geq \ \psi.$$

Both conditions imply $w > w_0$ as required by our assumption that the agent will conceal conflicting information. However, the restriction $x < \frac{1}{2}$ disappears.

As before, when the agent is not protected by limited liability, we could find a contract that implements the first best. Similarly, an example of an optimal contract when there is limited liability is

$$w_0 \ = \ 0$$
$$w \ = \ \frac{\psi}{x(1-x)}.$$

The rents left to the agent are now

$$\frac{\psi x}{1 - x}.$$

Notice that (given the previous assumptions) allowing the agent not to disclose evidence allows us to find an incentive compatible contract whichever the value of $p\beta$. Moreover, the rents will be always smaller since

$$\frac{\psi x}{1 - x} < \frac{2\psi x}{1 - 2x}.$$

6.4 Question 24

A risk-averse entrepreneur [with strictly increasing utility function $u(\cdot)$] produces random output q, uniformly distributed on $[0, \overline{q}]$, with $\overline{q} > 0$. The entrepreneur wants to diversify risk by writing a risk-sharing contract with a risk-neutral financier (with initial wealth $W \geq \overline{q}$), specifying a transfer to the entrepreneur contingent on realized output.

Output is observable to the entrepreneur. It is also observable to the financier unless the entrepreneur falsifies her accounts. After observing the realization of q, the entrepreneur can produce a falsifed output report R at cost

$$\psi(q, R) = \frac{1}{4}(q - R) + \frac{1}{2}c(q - R)^2$$

where $c > 0$. Suppose that the entrepreneur is protected by limited liability and that her reservation utility $\overline{u}$ is higher than $\overline{q}/2$.

1. Characterize the first-best contract.

2. A contract with no output falsification is such that $R(q) = q$ for all $q \in [0, \overline{q}]$. Show that the first-best contract would lead to falsification. Derive the entrepreneur's equilibrium falsification in response to the first-best contract.

3. What is the optimal no-falsification contract? Show that the optimal contract with no falsification is linear in output q (hint: all incentive constraints are satisfied as long as the contract is locally incentive-compatible at any $q \in [0, \overline{q}]$).

4. Explain why a contract with falsification may dominate the optimal contract with no falsification when $c \longrightarrow +\infty$.

Chapter 7

Bilateral Trading and Auctions

7.1 Question 25

Consider a public-good problem represented by a decision $d \in [0,1]$. Decision d has an impact on N individuals: Individual $i = 1, 2, ..., N$ has (differentiable) utility function $v_i(d, \theta_i) - T_i$, where θ_i is a privately known parameter and T_i is the payment made by the individual to the "planner." The socially efficient decision is

$$d^*(\theta) = \arg\max \sum_i v_i(d, \theta_i)$$

where $\theta \equiv (\theta_1, ..., \theta_N)$.

1. Derive the "Groves mechanism," that is, the direct revelation mechanism that implements $d^*(\theta)$ as a *dominant strategy equilibrium*. Show that it is unique. To do this, show that social efficiency implies

$$\theta_i = \arg\max_{\tilde{\theta}_i} \sum_j v_j[d^*(\theta_{-i}, \tilde{\theta}_i), \theta_j]$$

   where $\tilde{\theta}_i$ is any announcement that individual i could make. Use this result and the IC constraint for individual i to derive the Groves mechanism as the solution of a differential equation, which is unique up to a constant.

2. Show that budget balance [i.e., $\sum_i T_i(\theta) = 0$ for all θ] in the Groves mechanism can be satisfied if and only if $d^*(\theta)$ is "$(n-1)$-separable." *[The question should read that budget balance in the Groves mechanism can be satisfied if and only if $\max \sum_{i=1}^{n} v_i[d(\theta), \theta_i]$ is $(n-1)$-separable. –CCES]* Note that a function $F(m)$, with $m \equiv (m_1, m_2, ..., m_n)$, is $(n-1)$-separable if and only if it can be written as

$$\sum_i F_i(m_{-i})$$

3. Rather than insisting on dominant-strategy implementation, focus on *Bayesian implementation*. Assume the θ_i's are distributed independently. Show that there always exists a budget-balancing mechanism that leads to truth telling as a Bayesian equilibrium. To do so, start with a Groves mechanism and redistribute the surplus/deficit among the agents so as to leave the IC constraints unaffected.

7.2   Question 26

Consider a continuum of sellers and a continuum of buyers, each of measure 1. Each seller owns initially one unit of the good. Seller valuations for that good (denoted by v_S) are i.i.d. on $[\underline{v}_S, \overline{v}_S]$ with density $f_S(v_S)$. Each buyer is potentially interested in buying one unit of the good. Buyer valuations (denoted by v_B) are i.i.d. on $[\underline{v}_B, \overline{v}_B]$ with density $f_B(v_B)$. Assume that $\underline{v}_B < \underline{v}_S$.

Call $x_S(v_S)$ the seller's probability of selling given an announced v_S, and $x_B(v_B)$ the buyer's probability of buying given an announced v_B. Call $T_S(v_S)$ the seller's payment (to a "planner") given an announced v_S, and $T_B(v_B)$ the buyer's payment (to a "planner") given an announced v_B. Consider the "Walrasian mechanism," defined by

$$x_S(v_S) = 1 \ \text{ and } \ T_S(v_S) = P \quad \text{ if } \ v_S \leq P$$

$$x_S(v_S) = 0 \ \text{ and } \ T_S(v_S) = 0 \quad \text{ if } \ v_S > P$$

$$x_B(v_B) = 1 \ \text{ and } \ T_B(v_B) = -P \quad \text{ if } \ v_B \geq P$$

$$x_B(v_B) = 0 \ \text{ and } \ T_B(v_B) = 0 \quad \text{ if } \ v_B < P$$

1. Show that the IC constraints and IR constraints are satisfied for any price P.

2. Show that there exists a price P such that trade is efficient and balancedness is satisfied.

3. Compare with the Myerson-Satterthwaite (1983) result.

7.2.1   IC and IR Constraints

The seller's (IC) constraint is

$$T_s\left(v_s\right) + \left[1 - x_s\left(v_s\right)\right] v_s \geq T_s\left(\widehat{v}_s\right) + \left[1 - x_s\left(\widehat{v}_s\right)\right] v_s \text{ for any } \widehat{v}_s.$$

If $v_s \leq P$, the constraint holds with equality for any $\widehat{v}_s$ below P, and it holds with inequality for any $\widehat{v}_s$ above P. A similar argument can be made for $v_s > P$ to show the constraint is satisfied. This argument holds for any P.

The buyer's (IC) constraint is

$$T_b\left(v_b\right) + x_b\left(v_b\right) v_b \geq T_b\left(\widehat{v}_b\right) + x_b\left(\widehat{v}_b\right) v_b \text{ for any } \widehat{v}_b.$$

If $v_b \geq P$, the constraint holds with equality for any $\widehat{v}_b$ at or above P, and it holds with inequality for any $\widehat{v}_b$ below P. A similar argument can be made for $v_b < P$ to show the constraint is satisfied. Again, this argument holds for any P.

The seller's (IR) constraint is

$$T_s\left(v_s\right) + \left[1 - x_s\left(v_s\right)\right] v_s \geq 0 \text{ for any } v_s.$$

The buyer's (IR) constraint is

$$T_b\left(v_b\right) + x_b\left(v_b\right) v_b \geq 0 \text{ for any } v_b.$$

These are both satisfied because the seller only sells when the price is above her valuation and the buyer only buys when the price is below his valuation.

7.2.2 Efficient Trade

Efficient trade requires the buyers with the highest valuations to buy and the sellers with the lowest valuations to sell. The optimal choice of P for the Walrasian mechanism is given by the solution to

$$\max_{P} \int_{P}^{\overline{v}_b} \left[v_b - P\right] f_b\left(v_b\right) dv_b + \int_{\underline{v}_s}^{P} \left[P - v_s\right] f_s\left(v_s\right) dv_s.$$

Using Leibniz's Rule to take first order conditions we find

$$\int_{P}^{\overline{v}_b} -f_b\left(v_b\right) dv_b + \int_{\underline{v}_s}^{P} f_s\left(v_s\right) dv_s = 0$$

$\Leftrightarrow$

$$F_b\left(P\right) - 1 + F_s\left(P\right) = 0$$

$\Leftrightarrow$

$$F_s\left(P\right) = 1 - F_b\left(P\right).$$

The maximum is achieved by any P which solves this equation. We see immediately that balancedness is satisfied by the definition of the Walrasian mechanism since the price is the same for everyone. Efficiency is also achieved since the lowest valuation sellers trade with the highest valuation buyers up until the point where sellers value the good more than buyers. To see that efficiency implies this, consider maximizing the change in surplus though trade

$$\max \int_{\underline{v}_b}^{\overline{v}_b} v_b x_b\left(v_b\right) f_b\left(v_b\right) dv_b - \int_{\underline{v}_s}^{\overline{v}_s} v_s x_s\left(v_s\right) f_s\left(v_s\right) dv_s$$

subject to the constraints

$$\int_{\underline{v}_b}^{\overline{v}_b} x_b\left(v_b\right) f_b\left(v_b\right) dv_b = \int_{\underline{v}_s}^{\overline{v}_s} x_s\left(v_s\right) f_s\left(v_s\right) dv_s$$

$$0 \leq x_b\left(v_b\right) \leq 1$$

$$0 \leq x_s\left(v_s\right) \leq 1.$$

Clearly it is optimal to allow the low-value sellers and high-value buyers to trade first so solving this problem is equivalent to choosing the limits of integration $\widetilde{v}_s$ and $\widetilde{v}_b$ such that they solve

$$\max_{\widetilde{v}_s,\widetilde{v}_b} \int_{\widetilde{v}_b}^{\overline{v}_b} v_b f_b\left(v_b\right) dv_b - \int_{\underline{v}_s}^{\widetilde{v}_s} v_s f_s\left(v_s\right) dv_s$$

subject to

$$\int_{\widetilde{v}_b}^{\overline{v}_b} f_b\left(v_b\right) dv_b = \int_{\underline{v}_s}^{\widetilde{v}_s} f_s\left(v_s\right) dv_s.$$

Taking first order conditions with respect to $\widetilde{v}_s$ and $\widetilde{v}_b$ we find

$$\widetilde{v}_b f_b\left(\widetilde{v}_b\right) + \lambda f_b\left(\widetilde{v}_b\right) = 0$$
$$-\widetilde{v}_s f_s\left(\widetilde{v}_s\right) - \lambda f_s\left(\widetilde{v}_s\right) = 0.$$

Solving and using the constraint we have

$$\widetilde{v}_s = \widetilde{v}_b = P$$

$\Rightarrow$

$$\int_{\underline{v}_s}^{P} f_s\left(v_s\right) dv_s = \int_{P}^{\overline{v}_b} f_b\left(v_b\right) dv_b$$

$\Leftrightarrow$

$$F_s\left(P\right) = 1 - F_b\left(P\right)$$

which is the optimal P of our Walrasian mechanism.

7.2.3　Comparison with Myerson-Satterthwaite Theorem

Myerson & Satterthwaite (1983) establish that efficient trade cannot be achieved (there is no single price P) if contracting occurs at the interim stage between two agents with private information. The similarities with the above analysis are that there is a distribution of types and both (IC) and (IR) constraints are the same, that is, agents know their valuation when contracting takes place. The difference between the analyses is that the contract specified in Myerson & Satterthwaite is to facilitate trade between two specific types v_1 and v_2 which are unknown from a distribution of possible types. In contrast, in the analysis above, although the type of any one individual is unknown, there is a known continuum of individuals who exist and thus the amount of trade is fully known in advance.

The efficient outcome in our analysis is easily achieved, as we saw with the simple Walrasian mechanism analyzed. It is only important, so far as implementing the optimal mechanism, to determine whether an agent belongs in the group who should trade or not (that is, if $v_b > P$ and $v_s < P$). In the optimal mechanism an individual's announcement determines whether they will trade or not regardless of anybody else's announcement since the continuum of types which exist is known. In contrast, in Myerson & Satterthwaite it is important that an agent reveals his exact type since the types of the two agents are unknown and together determine whether trade should occur (that is, if $v_b > v_s$). Although this condition for trade is implied by the condition $v_b > P$ and $v_s < P$, the opposite is not true since $P > v_b > v_s$ or $v_b > v_s > P$ may be true.

7.3 Question 27

A decision where to locate a hazardous waste dump is taken through an auction between n towns in a given country. Call d_i town i's disutility from taking on the dump. Assume the d_i's are uniformly and independently distributed on $[0, 1]$. Call T_i the transfer the town requests from taking the hazardous waste dump. The lowest bidder gets the dump and receives its requested transfer, which is paid equally from the other towns. Compute the symmetric equilibrium of this auction. Is this an efficient allocation mechanism? Discuss.

7.4 Question 28

Consider a two-person, independent private-value auction with valuations uniformly distributed on $[0, 1]$. Compare the following assumptions on utilities: (a) bidder i ($i = 1, 2$) has utility $v_i - P$ when she wins the object and has to pay P, while her outside option is normalized to zero; (b) bidder i ($i = 1, 2$) has utility $\sqrt{v_i - P}$ when she wins the object and has to pay P, while her outside option is normalized to zero.

1. Compare the seller's expected revenue in cases (a) and (b) for the Vickrey auction.

2. Compare the seller's expected revenue in cases (a) and (b) for the (linear) symmetric bidding equilibrium of the first-price, sealed-bid auction.

3. Discuss.

7.5 Question 29

Consider an auction setting where a risk-neutral seller of a house faces two potential risk-neutral buyers. Buyer 1 is a real-estate agent who knows the market value of the house perfectly. Buyer 2 does not know the market value of the house, and the same goes for the seller. The seller is determined to sell the house, while each buyer is uninterested in buying at a price higher than the expected value of the house. The value of the house v is either v_H or v_L with $v_H > v_L$, and the seller's and buyer 2's ex ante beliefs are given by $\beta \equiv \Pr(v = v_L)$. Except for the realization of v, all the preceding information is common knowledge.

1. Show that buyer 2 obtains an expected payoff of zero in the first-price sealed-bid auction.

2. Which of the following standard auctions maximizes the seller's expected revenue: the English, Vickrey, or Dutch auction?

3. What is the optimal auction?

4. Assuming now that v is uniformly distributed on the interval $[0, 1]$, characterize the Bayesian equilibrium in the first-price sealed-bid auction. What is the equilibrium payoff of the uninformed buyer?

7.5.1 Expected Payoff

We assume in this question that if two parties make the same bid then each wins the auction with probability $\frac{1}{2}$. We proceed with a proof by contradiction and assume the expected payoff to player 2 is greater than 0.

Define strategies for buyer 1 as follows:

$$b(v_L) = \arg\max_b (v_L - b)g(b)$$
$$b(v_H) = \arg\max_b (v_H - b)g(b)$$

where $g(b)$ is the probability of winning when bidding b against the potentially mixed strategy of buyer 2.

Now it must be the case that the informed bidder bids $b(v_L) = v_L$. Suppose that part of the support of buyer 2's strategy lies below v_L, otherwise buyer 1 never wins when $v = v_L$ and is indifferent between bidding anything less than or equal to v_L. Buyer 1 can earn a positive expected return by simply bidding $v_L - \varepsilon$ and must win at least some of the time. If this is the case then the part of the support less than $b(v_L)$ never wins and in order for it to be part of the support it must win at least some of the time. The mass located at this point must shift up to at least $b(v_L)$. This in turn then pushes up $b(v_L)$ and it increases in this Bertrand manner until we have $b(v_L) = v_L$.

The support of buyer 2's mixed strategy must lie strictly between v_L and $\beta(v_H - v_L) + v_L$. If buyer 1 is bidding $b(v_L) = v_L$, then v_L cannot be in the support of buyer 2's mixed strategy, since making such a bid would give an expected return of 0. Since $b(v_H) > v_L$ the buyer would only win when the good is of low value. Nor can the buyer bid more than $\beta(v_H - v_L) + v_L$ since this is the ex ante expected value of the house.

We can now present the contradiction. Buyer 1 must win some of the time when the house is of high value and thus $\Pr(b(v_H) \geq b_U) > 0$. This implies one of the following:

- buyer 2 has a mass of probability at $b(v_H)$, or

- there is a positive probability that buyer 2 bids strictly less than b_U.

However, neither of these can be true. In the first case buyer 1 would prefer to choose $b(v_H) + \varepsilon$ and $b(v_H)$ is not buyer 1's optimal bid. In the second case these bids can only win when $v = v_L$ and the expected return from making these bids is smaller or equal to 0. This cannot be true because it implies the expected payoff of the mixed strategy is ≤ 0. Thus we have a contradiction and it must be the case that the expected payoff of the uninformed bidder is 0.

7.5.2 Standard Auctions

Assumptions are needed to determine the auction which maximizes the seller's expected revenue.

For the English auction, the full market value may be extracted if we assume that the uninformed buyer can infer the value of the house from the bidding behavior of the informed buyer. Such is the case in an equilibrium where the informed bidder drops out at v_L if the market value is v_L (he is indifferent to doing so) and thus the uninformed bidder can infer the value, and bid up to v_H if the informed bidder is still bidding at v_L. If, however, we assume that this is not the case, and the uninformed bidder has to decide whether to continue at v_L, then the uninformed bidder will drop out at v_L, since he knows that he cannot win at a price lower than the market value and if he continues to $v_L + \varepsilon$ he could lose. In this case the English auction only yields an expected (and actual) revenue of v_L.

For the Vickrey auction we must also distinguish between two equilibria. It is always a dominant strategy for the informed to bid his valuation (as in the case of a second price sealed bid). However, knowing this, the uninformed may bid v_L or v_H. There is no winner's curse in this situation since the uninformed knows that, given the informed party's strategy, even when he bids v_H he will not overpay for the house. In the equilibrium where the uninformed always bids v_H the Vickrey is equivalent to the equilibrium in the English auction where there seller extracts the full market value of the house. However, in the equilibrium where the uninformed always bids v_L the seller will always receive v_L.

In the Dutch auction the informed buyer has a strict incentive to allow the price to fall below v_H when it is high-valued to try and extract some surplus (as is the case in the first price sealed bid auction). The uninformed buyer knows this so when the price falls below v_H she does not learn anything about the value of the house and is unwilling to buy it while the price is above her ex ante expected value. Buyer 1 knows this so will never purchase the house for a price greater than $\beta(v_H - v_L) + v_L + \varepsilon$. The only way this auction can raise as much revenue as the English is if the house is sold for $\beta(v_H - v_L) + v_L$ all the time. When $v = v_L$ buyer 1 will not bid more than this so to achieve this outcome the equilibrium must involve buyer 2 bidding $\beta(v_H - v_L) + v_L$ all the time. However, the winner's curse will preclude this from happening because buyer 1's optimal strategy will be to simply buy the house for $\beta(v_H - v_L) + v_L + \varepsilon$ when $v = v_H$ and allow buyer 2 to purchase it at $\beta(v_H - v_L) + v_L$ when $v = v_L$ so that buyer 2 would make a negative expected payoff from such a strategy. Thus, given the randomization, the Dutch will be inferior to the English and Vickrey in the equilibria where the seller extracts the full market value, and superior to the Vickrey and English in the equilibria where the seller gets v_L.

7.5.3   Optimal Auction

The optimal auction specifies payments $P_I(v)$ and $P_U(v)$ and probabilities $x_I(v)$ and $x_U(v)$, for the informed and uninformed buyers respectively, conditional on the informed agent's announced valuation v. The optimal auction will always result in the house being sold so $x_I(v_i) = 1 - x_U(v_i)$ for $i = H, L$. Applying the revelation principle we can restrict our attention to contracts where the informed agent always truthfully reveals the value of the house and both agents' (IC) and (IR) constraints are satisfied. The optimal contract is one which sets $x_I(v_H) = 1$, $x_U(v_H) = 0$, $P_I(v_H) = v_H$, $P_U(v) = 0$ and $x_U(v_L) = 1$, $x_I(v_L) = 0$, $P_U(v_L) = v_L$, $P_I(v_L) = 0$.

7.5.4   Uniform Distribution

Here we guess and verify. We can characterize the equilibrium by assuming the following: the uninformed buyer uses a mixed strategy, the informed buyer uses a bidding function $b_I(v)$ such that $\frac{\partial b_I}{\partial v} > 0$, and the support of the uninformed buyer's mixed strategy and the range of the informed buyer's bidding function are the same. These assumptions come from our analysis in the first part.

We can determine the bidding function of the informed buyer by first observing that the uninformed buyer has an expected payoff of 0. If she wins the auction with a bid equal to α, which can be mapped to a value of the buyer's bidding function $b_I(v)$, then, using the indifference condition of the mixed strategy of the uninformed bidder, the bidding function $b_I(v)$ must satisfy

$$\left[\frac{v_i}{2} - b_I(v_i)\right] v_i = 0 \text{ for all } v.$$

This implies

$$b_I(v_i) = \frac{v_i}{2} \text{ for } v_i \in [0, 1]$$

where $\frac{v_i}{2}$ is the expected value of the house given that the uninformed buyer has won the auction with a bid of $b_I(v_i)$, v_i is then the probability that the realized bid from the informed buyer $b_I(v)$ is below the bid $b_I(v_i)$. We see that the informed buyer bids half her valuation. We can solve for the mixed strategy of the uninformed buyer. The informed buyer's choice of b given v_i satisfies

$$b_I(v_i) = \frac{v_i}{2} = \arg\max_b F_U(b)\left[v_i - b_I(v_i)\right] \text{ for each } v_i.$$

Taking the first order conditions

$$F_U'(b)\left[v_i - b_I(v_i)\right] - F_U(b) = 0$$
$$v_i - b_I(v_i) = \frac{F_U(b)}{F_U'(b)}$$

substituting in $v_i = 2b_I(v_i)$

$$
\begin{aligned}
b_I(v_i) &= \frac{F_U(b)}{F'_U(b)} \\
&\Rightarrow F_U(b) = 2b \\
&\Rightarrow f_U(b) = 2.
\end{aligned}
$$

The uninformed buyer has a uniform mixed strategy over the interval $\left[0, \frac{1}{2}\right]$.

Chapter 8

Multiagent Moral Hazard and Collusion

8.1 Question 30

Consider a risk-neutral principal who employs two agents, $i = 1, 2$, who can produce an amount $q_i = f(a_i, \varepsilon_i)$, where a_i is agent i's effort level and ε_i is a random shock with (atomless) density $g(\varepsilon_i)$. The ε_i's are identically and independently distributed. Each agent has outside opportunity level of utility normalized to zero. Agents are not wealth constrained.

1. Assume first that each agent i is risk neutral, with utility equal to monetary compensation, w_i, minus a convex cost of effort $\psi(a_i)$. Assuming that a positive level of production is desirable, derive the first-best outcome where each agent has a zero expected payoff. Show how it can be achieved through an incentive scheme where each agent is rewarded according to her output only. Show how it can also be achieved (assuming that a symmetric pure-strategy Nash equilibrium exists) through a simple tournament where the agent who is "behind" in terms of individual output is paid an amount W_l and the one who is "ahead" is paid an amount W_w. Discuss.

2. Assume now that each agent i is risk averse, with utility equal to $u(w_i) - \psi(a_i)$, where $u(\cdot)$ is strictly increasing and concave. Extend the class of possible relative-performance incentive schemes to $W_1(q_1, q_2)$ and $W_2(q_1, q_2)$. Consider any pair (a_1, a_2) that can be sustained as a Nash equilibrium as a result of these incentive schemes and that also give each agent a nonnegative expected utility level. Show that this pair of effort levels can also be sustained in this way by a pair of incentive schemes $W_1(q_1)$ and $W_2(q_2)$ that lacks relative performance evaluation and that does not have a higher expected cost for the principal. Discuss.

8.1.1   Attaining the First Best Under Risk Neutrality

We first derive the efficient levels of effort a_1^* and a_2^*. Given that the disturbance terms are independent, the two agents can be treated separately. Moreover, given that the two agents are identical, the efficient contract will be the same. For $i = 1, 2$ we have

$$\max_{a_i} \int [f(a_i, \varepsilon_i) - \psi(a_i)] \, g(\varepsilon_i) \, d\varepsilon_i.$$

The first order condition is

$$\int f_{a_i}(a_i^*, \varepsilon_i) g(\varepsilon_i) \, d\varepsilon_i = \psi'(a_i^*).$$

When $f(a_i, \varepsilon_i) = a_i + \varepsilon_i$, as in Lazear and Rosen (1981), the left hand side simplifies to 1.

Piece Rates

Here, the intuition is clear. The risk-neutral agent will bear all the risk by keeping the output q_i he produces and paying $\int [f(a_i^*, \varepsilon_i) - \psi(a_i^*)] \, g(\varepsilon_i) \, d\varepsilon_i$ up front to the principal. Note that a_i^* solves

$$\max_{a_i} \int [f(a_i, \varepsilon_i) - \psi(a_i)] \, g(\varepsilon_i) \, d\varepsilon_i - \int [f(a_i^*, \varepsilon_i) - \psi(a_i^*)] \, g(\varepsilon_i) \, d\varepsilon_i$$

and that at this optimum the agent expects a payoff equal to zero. The incentives to expend costly effort come from making the reward dependent on the level of individual production.

Tournament

In a tournament, in contrast with piece rates, costly effort is induced through the prize gap between the winner and loser of the tournament. The agents can increase the probability of winning the higher prize by exerting additional effort. Given the effort choice of the opponent, every agent solves

$$\max_{a_i} \Pr(f(a_i, \varepsilon_i) > f(a_{-i}^{**}, \varepsilon_{-i})) \, [W_w - W_l] + W_l - \psi(a_i).$$

Assuming that a symmetric pure-strategy Nash equilibrium exists with $a_i^{**} = a_{-i}^{**}$, it is characterized by

$$\frac{d \Pr(f(a_i^{**}, \varepsilon_i) > f(a_{-i}^{**}, \varepsilon_{-i}))}{da_i} [W_w - W_l] = \psi'(a_i^{**}) \text{ for } i = 1, 2.$$

The difference in prizes $W_w - W_l$ can be set such that the efficient effort level $a_i^{**} = a_i^*$ will be chosen. The level of the prizes can be set to extract all rents from the agents such that again each agent has a zero expected payoff.

With $f(a_i, \varepsilon_i) = a_i + \varepsilon_i$, the left hand side simplifies to

$$\frac{d}{da_i} \Pr(\varepsilon_i - \varepsilon_{-i} > a_{-i}^{**} - a_i)\big|_{a_i = a_i^{**}} = \frac{d}{da_i} \Pr(\varepsilon_i - \varepsilon_{-i} > 0).$$

To induce the efficient effort level, the principal sets

$$W_w - W_l = \frac{\psi'(a^*)}{\frac{d}{da_i} \Pr(\varepsilon_i - \varepsilon_{-i} > 0)}.$$

8.1.2 Risk Aversion

Given performance scheme $W_i(q_i, q_{-i})$ and expected effort level of the opponent a_{-i}, agent i chooses

$$a_i \in \arg\max_{\hat{a}_i} \int \int u(W_i(f(\hat{a}_i, \varepsilon_i), f(a_{-i}, \varepsilon_{-i}))) g(\varepsilon_{-i}) g(\varepsilon_i) d\varepsilon_{-i} d\varepsilon_i - \psi(\hat{a}_i)$$

with first order condition

$$E_{\varepsilon_i, \varepsilon_{-i}}[u'(W_i(q_i, q_{-i})) \frac{\partial}{\partial q_i} W_i(q_i, q_{-i}) \frac{\partial}{\partial a_i} f(a_i, \varepsilon_i)] = \psi'(a_i). \qquad \text{(IC)}$$

This performance scheme satisfies the participation constraint if

$$E_{\varepsilon_i, \varepsilon_{-i}} u(W_i(f(a_i, \varepsilon_i), f(a_{-i}, \varepsilon_{-i}))) \geq \psi(a_i) \qquad \text{(IR)}$$

holds.

So the set of pairs (a_1, a_2), for which the expected utility level is non-negative and that can be sustained as a Nash equilibrium given a pair of incentive schemes $W_1(q_1, q_2)$ and $W_2(q_1, q_2)$, are described by

$$A = \{(a_1, a_2) \,|\, \exists W_1(q_1, q_2), W_2(q_1, q_2) \text{ such that}$$
$$\text{condition (IC) and (IR) hold for } i = 1, 2\}.$$

Here we have used relative performance schemes to induce agents to expend the desired level of efforts. However, we know from Holmstrom (1982b) that when the output shocks of the agents are independent (no common shock has to be filtered out), there is no reason for introducing a form of relative performance evaluation. Hence, one can do at least as well with a pair of incentive schemes that lacks relative performance evaluation.

Using the independence of the random terms, we rewrite the maximization problem solved by each agent as

$$\max_{\hat{a}_i} \int \left[\int u(W_i(f(\hat{a}_i, \varepsilon_i), f(a_{-i}, \varepsilon_{-i}))) g(\varepsilon_{-i}) d\varepsilon_{-i} \right] g(\varepsilon_i) d\varepsilon_i - \psi(\hat{a}_i).$$

For a given a_{-i}, we can find $\tilde{W}_i(\cdot)$ such that the term between squared brackets can be rewritten as $u(\tilde{W}_i(f(\hat{a}_i, \varepsilon_i)))$. Therefore, the problem is equivalent to

$$\max_{\hat{a}_i} \int u(\tilde{W}_i(f(\hat{a}_i, \varepsilon_i))) g(\varepsilon_i) d\varepsilon_i - \psi(\hat{a}_i)$$

with first order condition

$$E_{\varepsilon_i}[u'(\tilde{W}_i(q_i))\tilde{W}_i'(q_i)\frac{\partial}{\partial a_i}f(a_i,\varepsilon_i)] = \psi'(a_i).   \quad\text{(IC')}$$

The participation constraint can be rewritten as

$$E_{\varepsilon_i}u(\tilde{W}_i(q_i)) \geq \psi(a_i).   \quad\text{(IR')}$$

So any pair of efforts (a_1, a_2) in A can be implemented by a pair of incentive schemes

$$u(\tilde{W}_i(f(a_i,\varepsilon_i))) = \int u(W_i(f(a_i,\varepsilon_i), f(a_{-i},\varepsilon_{-i})))g(\varepsilon_{-i})d\varepsilon_{-i} \text{ for } i = 1, 2 \ ,$$

because the pair satisfies conditions (IC') and (IR') which are equivalent to (IC) and (IR) respectively. Furthermore, the concavity of the utility function implies that

$$\tilde{W}_i(f(a_i,\varepsilon_i))) \leq \int W_i(f(a_i,\varepsilon_i), f(a_{-i},\varepsilon_{-i}))g(\varepsilon_{-i})d\varepsilon_{-i} \text{ for } i = 1, 2.$$

When the agents' output shocks are independent, relative performance evaluation introduces extra risk in the incentive scheme for which the principal needs to compensate the agents. Hence, the expected cost for the principal will be lower for the incentive scheme without relative performance evaluation.

8.2   Question 31

Two agents can work for a principal. The output of agent i, $i = 1, 2$, is $q_i = a_i + \varepsilon_i$, where a_i is agent i's effort level and ε_i is a random shock. The ε_i's are independent of each other and normally distributed with mean 0 and variance σ^2.

In addition to choosing a_2, agent 2 can engage in a second activity b_2. This activity does not affect output directly, but rather reduces the effort cost of agent 1. The interpretation is that agent 2 can *help* agent 1 (but not the other way around). The cost functions of the agents are

$$\psi_1(a_1, b_2) = \frac{1}{2}(a_1 - b_2)^2$$

and

$$\psi_2(a_2, b_2) = \frac{1}{2}a_2^2 + b_2^2.$$

Agent 1 chooses her effort level a_1 only after she has observed the level of help b_2. Agent i's utility function is exponential and equal to

$$-e^{[-\eta(w_i - \psi_i(a_i, b_2))]}$$

where w_i is the agent's income. The agent's reservation utility is -1, which corresponds to a reservation wage of 0. The principal is risk neutral and is restricted to linear incentive schemes. The incentive scheme for agent i is

$$w_i = z_i + v_i q_i + u_i q_j$$

1. Assume that a_1, a_2, and b_2 are observable. Solve the principal's problem by maximizing the total expected surplus with respect to a_1, a_2, and b_2. Explain why $a_1 > a_2$.

2. Assume from now on that a_1, a_2, and b_2 are not observable. Solve again the principal's problem. Explain why $u_1 = 0$.

3. Assume that the principal cannot distinguish whether a unit of output was produced by agent 1 or agent 2. The agents can thus engage in *arbitrage*, claiming that all output was produced by one of them. Assume that they will do so whenever it increases the sum of their wages. Explain why the incentive scheme in part 2 above leads to arbitrage. What additional constraint does arbitrage impose on the principal's problem? Solve this problem, and explain why $u_1 > 0$.

8.3 Question 32

Two agents work for a principal. The output of agent i, $i = 1, 2$, is $q_i = a_i + \varepsilon_i$, where a_i is agent i's (privately observed) effort level and ε_i is a random shock. The ε_i's are normally distributed with mean 0 and variance-covariance matrix:

$$\begin{pmatrix} 1 & \rho \\ \rho & 1 \end{pmatrix}$$

Agent i's utility function is:

$$-e^{\left[-\eta \left(w_i - \frac{c}{2} a_i^2 \right) \right]}$$

where w_i is the agent's income. Each agent's reservation wage is 0. The principal is risk-neutral and is restricted to (symmetric) linear incentive schemes. Specifically, the incentive scheme for agent i is

$$w_i = z + v q_i + u q_j$$

Agents can collude by writing a side contract before efforts are chosen. Assume agent 1 can make the following take-it-or-leave-it contract offer to agent 2

$$s = \phi(q_1 - q_2) + \varphi$$

1. Derive the optimal side-contract for an arbitrary incentive scheme (v, u), assuming that effort choices cannot be part of the side contract.

2. Show that the principal can without loss of generality restrict attention to collusion-proof contracts.

3. Derive the optimal collusion-proof contract. Discuss.

4. Would the principal benefit if collusion were made impossible? How would the answer change if agents could write a side contract conditional on effort choices?

8.3.1 Optimal Side Contract

The agents' certainty equivalents for given incentive and side contracts are

$$CE_1 = z + va_1 + ua_2 - \phi(a_1 - a_2) - \varphi$$
$$- \frac{\eta}{2} \left[(v - \phi)^2 + (u + \phi)^2 + 2\rho(v - \phi)(u + \phi) \right] - \frac{c}{2} a_1^2$$

$$CE_2 = z + va_2 + ua_1 + \phi(a_1 - a_2) + \varphi$$
$$- \frac{\eta}{2} \left[(v - \phi)^2 + (u + \phi)^2 + 2\rho(v - \phi)(u + \phi) \right] - \frac{c}{2} a_2^2.$$

Since φ can be used as a transfer between the two agents to satisfy agent 2's participation constraint, the maximization problem for agent 1 can be rewritten as a joint maximization problem for both agents:

$$\max_{\phi} CE_1 + CE_2$$

subject to

$$a_1 \in \arg\max CE_1$$
$$a_2 \in \arg\max CE_2$$
$$CE_2(\phi, \varphi) \geq CE_2(\phi = 0, \varphi = 0).$$

The agents' first order conditions yield

$$a_1 = a_2 = \frac{v - \phi}{c}.$$

The problem is therefore given by

$$\max_{\phi} 2z + 2 \frac{(v + u)(v - \phi)}{c}$$
$$- \eta \left[(v - \phi)^2 + (u + \phi)^2 + 2\rho(v - \phi)(u + \phi) \right] - c \left(\frac{v - \phi}{c} \right)^2.$$

From the first order conditions we obtain

$$-2 \frac{v + u}{c} - \eta \left[-2(v - \phi) + 2(u + \phi) + 2\rho(v - \phi) - 2\rho(u + \phi) \right] + 2 \frac{v - \phi}{c} = 0$$

which after some re-arranging simplifies to

$$\phi = \frac{\eta c(1 - \rho)(v - u) - u}{1 + 2\eta c(1 - \rho)}.$$

Finally, as mentioned above, φ is chosen to just satisfy agent 2's participation constraint

$$z + \varphi + \frac{(v + u)(v - \phi)}{c} - \frac{c}{2}\left(\frac{v - \phi}{c}\right)^2$$
$$- \frac{\eta}{2}\left[(v - \phi)^2 + (u + \phi)^2 + 2\rho(v - \phi)(u + \phi)\right]$$
$$\geq z + \frac{(v + u)v}{c} - \frac{c}{2}\left(\frac{v}{c}\right)^2 - \frac{\eta}{2}\left[v^2 + u^2 + 2\rho vu\right].$$

Rearranging and letting the constraint bind we find

$$\varphi = \frac{\phi(2u + \phi)}{2c} + \eta\phi(1 - \rho)(u - v + \phi).$$

8.3.2   Restriction to Collusion-Proof Contracts

Suppose that the principal has offered the agents the contract (z, v, u) and, conditional on these contracts, the agents write an optimal side contract (φ, ϕ). This means that there is no other side contract which the agents would find more desirable. Now, suppose that the principal instead were to offer the agents the contracts $(z + \varphi, v - \phi, u + \phi)$ and $(z - \varphi, v - \phi, u + \phi)$. Since this puts the agents in the same position as they were in the initial scenario after side contracting, by revealed preference, the agents will be satisfied not to side contract under the new scheme. Hence, since the principal can always undo the side contract she can restrict herself to collusion-proof contracts. Note, however, that this approach forces the principal into a more restricted problem.

8.3.3   Optimal Collusion-Proof Contract

The principal solves the following maximization problem

$$\max_{a_1, a_2, z, v, u} E\pi = (a_1 + a_2)(1 - u - v) - 2z$$

subject to

$$CE_1 \geq 0$$
$$CE_2 \geq 0$$

and

$$a_1 \in \arg\max CE_1$$
$$a_2 \in \arg\max CE_2$$

as well as subject to the collusion-proofness constraint

$$\phi = 0.$$

From before we know that under the optimal side contract the agents will set $\phi = \frac{\eta c(1-\rho)(v-u)-u}{1+2\eta c(1-\rho)}$. As a result, under a collusion-proof contract the principal will set

$$v = \frac{1 + \eta c(1 - \rho)}{\eta c(1 - \rho)} u = \tau u$$

where $\tau = \frac{1+\eta c(1-\rho)}{\eta c(1-\rho)} > 1$. Furthermore, from the incentive compatibility constraints we know that

$$a_1 = a_2 = \frac{v}{c}.$$

Finally, noting that the participation constraints are binding, we can rewrite the maximization problem as

$$\max_{v,u} E\pi = 2\frac{v}{c} - \frac{v^2}{c} - \eta(v^2 + u^2 + 2\rho vu).$$

Substituting for v we have

$$\max_{u} E\pi = 2\frac{\tau u}{c} - \frac{\tau^2 u^2}{c} - \eta(\tau^2 u^2 + u^2 + 2\rho\tau u^2)$$

from which we obtain first order conditions with respect to u

$$2\frac{\tau}{c} - 2\frac{\tau^2}{c}u - \eta(2\tau^2 u + 2u + 4\rho\tau u) = 0.$$

The optimal collusion-proof contract is therefore given by

$$u = \frac{\tau}{\tau^2 + \eta c(\tau^2 + 2\rho\tau + 1)}$$

$$v = \frac{\tau^2}{\tau^2 + \eta c(\tau^2 + 2\rho\tau + 1)}$$

and z is again set to satisfy the participation constraints. The principal's profit is given by

$$E\pi^{side} = \frac{\tau}{c}u = \frac{\tau^2}{[\tau^2 + \eta c(\tau^2 + 2\rho\tau + 1)]c}.$$

As mentioned before the principal is forced to set $v = \tau u$ in order to rule out collusion between the agents who would otherwise use a side contract to equalize effective incentives. This severely limits the principal's ability to use a more fine-tuned relative performance evaluation scheme that would better exploit the correlation in the error structure.

8.3.4   Collusion Impossible

If collusion is made impossible the principal solves the following problem:

$$\max_{a_1,a_2,z,v,u} E\pi = (a_1 + a_2)(1 - u - v) - 2z$$

subject to

$$CE_1 \geq 0$$
$$CE_2 \geq 0$$

and

$$a_1 \in \arg\max CE_1$$
$$a_2 \in \arg\max CE_2.$$

Note that in this case, in contrast to the previous situation, the principal does not have to worry about the additional collusion-proofness constraint.

Using the participation and incentive compatibility constraints the principal's objective function can be rewritten as

$$\max_{v,u} E\pi = 2\frac{v}{c} - \eta(v^2 + u^2 + 2\rho uv) - \frac{v^2}{c}.$$

The principal's problem can be solved sequentially. First, for any given v, u is determined to minimize risk. Second, v is set optimally. Minimizing the variance with respect to u yields

$$u = -\rho v.$$

We substitute this expression into the principal's objective function to obtain

$$\max_{v} E\pi = 2\frac{v}{c} - \eta v^2(1 - \rho^2) - \frac{v^2}{c}$$

and consequently

$$v = \frac{1}{1 + \eta c(1 - \rho^2)}$$
$$u = -\frac{\rho}{1 + \eta c(1 - \rho^2)}.$$

As a result the expected profit for the principal when collusion is impossible is given by

$$E\pi^{no} = \frac{1}{[1 + \eta c(1 - \rho^2)]\, c}.$$

Clearly, it must be the case that

$$E\pi^{no} \geq E\pi^{side}.$$

We can verify this statement using our solutions

$$
\begin{aligned}
\frac{1}{[1+\eta c(1-\rho^2)]\,c} &\geq \frac{\tau^2}{[\tau^2+\eta c(\tau^2+2\rho\tau+1)]\,c} \\
\tau^2+\eta c(\tau^2+2\rho\tau+1) &\geq \tau^2\left[1+\eta c(1-\rho^2)\right] \\
\tau^2+2\rho\tau+1 &\geq \tau^2(1-\rho^2) \\
\tau^2\rho^2+2\rho\tau+1 &\geq 0 \\
(\tau\rho+1)^2 &\geq 0.
\end{aligned}
$$

More generally, the principal would benefit if collusion were made impossible since collusion-proofness forces the principal into a more restricted problem than the no-side-contracting problem. This is because the agents can only use the same information as the principal when writing their side contract.

Full Side Contracting

However, when the agents could write a side contract conditional on effort choices, then full side contracting dominates no side contracting if and only if $\rho \leq \bar{\rho}$. The advantage of relative performance evaluation is larger the larger the correlation ρ. However, while cooperation induces more effort due to the agents' monitoring of each other, it also undermines relative performance evaluation, raising the cost to the principal. As shown in section 8.2.2.2 the full side-contracting problem can be reduced to a single agent contracting problem where the principal faces a single agent with coefficient of risk aversion η_J defined by

$$
\frac{1}{\eta_J} = \frac{1}{\eta} + \frac{1}{\eta}
$$

and cost of effort function

$$
c(a_1, a_2) = \frac{c}{2}a_1^2 + \frac{c}{2}a_2^2.
$$

Clearly,

$$
\eta_J = \frac{\eta}{2}
$$

and so the agent's certainty equivalent is

$$
CE_J = z + va_1 + ua_2 - \frac{\eta}{4}(v^2 + u^2 + 2\rho uv) - \frac{c}{2}a_1^2 - \frac{c}{2}a_2^2.
$$

The principal's problem is

$$
\max_{a_1,a_2,z,v,u} \; E\pi = a_1(1-v) + a_2(1-u) - z
$$

subject to

$$
CE_J \geq 0
$$

and

$$
a_1, a_2 \in \arg\max CE_J.
$$

From the agent's first order conditions we obtain

$$a_1 = \frac{v}{c}$$
$$a_2 = \frac{u}{c}$$

and using the binding individual rationality constraint we have the following unconstrained problem

$$\max_{v,u} E\pi = \frac{v}{c} + \frac{u}{c} - \frac{\eta}{4}(v^2 + u^2 + 2\rho uv) - \frac{c}{2}\left[\left(\frac{v}{c}\right)^2 + \left(\frac{u}{c}\right)^2\right].$$

The first order conditions are

$$\frac{1}{c} - \frac{\eta}{2}(v + \rho u) - \frac{v}{c} = 0$$
$$\frac{1}{c} - \frac{\eta}{2}(u + \rho v) - \frac{u}{c} = 0$$

from which we obtain

$$u = v = \frac{2}{2 + \eta c(1 + \rho)}.$$

The principal's expected profit is

$$E\pi^{full} = \frac{2}{[2 + \eta c(1 + \rho)]\,c}.$$

Full side-contracting yields higher expected profits if and only if

$$E\pi^{full} \geq E\pi^{no}$$

$\Leftrightarrow$

$$\frac{2}{[2 + \eta c(1 + \rho)]\,c} \geq \frac{1}{[1 + \eta c(1 - \rho^2)]\,c}$$

$\Leftrightarrow$

$$\frac{1}{2} \geq \rho.$$

Thus if $\rho \leq \frac{1}{2} = \bar{\rho}$ full side contracting will be preferred to no side contracting.

8.4 Question 33

A (risk-neutral) municipal government considers funding an investment project put forward by an association (also risk-neutral). The cost of the project is known, but the government is unsure about its social value, and its assessment is at odds with that of the association. Specifically, if the project is of "good quality," its social value (net of the cost of the project) as assessed by the government is $\theta_G > 0$, while the association would derive a private benefit $v_G > 0$ from seeing it go through. If instead the project is of "bad quality," its net social value is $\theta_B < 0$, but the association would derive a private benefit v_B, higher than v_G, if it went through. The association knows the quality of the project, while the government's (common-knowledge) belief is $\Pr(v_B) = \beta$.

In the absence of information, the government is ready to fund the project, since we assume $\beta \theta_B + (1 - \beta)\theta_G > 0$. However, since taxation is distortionary, the government has net value $\lambda > 0$ for each unit of revenue raised from the association. However, the government would be unwilling to allow a bad-quality project to go through even if it were able to charge the association for its full private benefit; that is, we assume $\theta_B + \lambda v_B < 0$.

Assume the government has access to a (risk-neutral) "expert" who, when the project is of bad quality, manages to obtain an (unfalsifiable) proof of this fact with probability p, but observes "nothing" with probability $(1 - p)$; "nothing" is also observed with probability 1 when the project is of good quality. The expert starts with no financial resources and can therefore only be rewarded not punished. The association is assumed to observe when the expert obtains a proof of bad quality, while the government has to be "alerted" by the expert.

1. Derive first the optimal scheme for the government when it cannot rely at all on the expert.

2. What is the optimal scheme when the government can rely on the expert and when collusion between the expert and the association is impossible because the expert is "honest"?

3. What is the optimal scheme when the government can rely on the expert but the expert is "self-interested" and the association can promise the expert a side payment for not alerting the government when he obtains a proof of bad quality? Assume the collusion technology is such that, for every unit of money the association pays, the expert only collects an equivalent of $k < 1$ units of money.

4. What is the optimal scheme when the government is unsure about the prospect for collusion, because it believes that with probability γ the expert is "honest" and with probability $1 - \gamma$ it is "self-interested"?

Chapter 9

Dynamic Adverse Selection

9.1 Question 34

Consider a two-period durable-goods monopoly problem where a seller faces a single buyer with reservation utility for the durable good $v \in \{v_L, v_H\}$ with $v_H > v_L > 0$. The seller's prior belief about the buyer's reservation utility is $\Pr(v = v_H) = 0.5$. The seller's cost of producing the good can also take two equally likely values: $c \in \{c_L, c_H\}$ with $c_H > c_L \geq 0$. Seller costs and buyer reservation values are independently distributed and are private information. Assume

$$v_L - c_L \geq \frac{v_H - c_L}{2}$$

and

$$v_L - c_H < \frac{v_H - c_H}{2}$$

The common discount factor is given by $\delta > 0$. *[This question assumes that the valuation of the good if bought in the first period is v_i, whereas if bought in the second period it is δv_i, contrary to the setup in section 9.1. –CCES]*

1. Under what conditions does a pooling equilibrium exist in the first period where
   (a) both types of seller set a first-period price

   $$p_1 = v_H - \frac{\delta}{2}(v_H - v_L)$$

   (b) the type-v_H buyer accepts this price with probability

   $$\gamma = \frac{v_H + c_H - 2v_L}{v_H - v_L}$$

   and the type-v_L buyer rejects it with probability 1; and (c) following a period-1 rejection, the type-c_L seller sets $p_2^L = v_L$ in the second period and the type-c_H seller sets $p_2^H = v_H$ in the second period?

2. Explain why the seller gains from having private information about costs when his cost is c_L, but not when it is c_H.

9.2   Question 35

Consider a two-period regulation model where the "type" of the firm is endogenous. Initially, the regulator offers a revenue function $R_1(q)$ specifying the payment it offers for output level q. Then, the firm sinks a (privately observed) amount I that determines its per-period production cost $c(q, I)$ [with $c(0, I) = c_q(0, I) = 0, c_{qq}(q, I) > \varepsilon > 0$, and $c_I(q, I) < 0$], and chooses to produce quantity q_1, which leads to first-period payoff

$$R_1(q_1) - c(q_1, I) - I$$

If instead the firm quits, it earns $-I$ and the game is over. If the firm has chosen q_1, the regulator's first-period payoff is $q_1 - R_1(q_1)$.

In the second period, after having observed q_1, the regulator offers $R_2(q)$, upon which the firm either quits (leading to a zero payoff for both parties in period 2) or chooses q_2, with associated second-period payoffs $R_2(q_2) - c(q_2, I)$ and $q_2 - R_2(q_2)$ for the two parties.

1. What is the full-commitment strategy of the regulator?

2. In the absence of commitment, show that this game has no pure-strategy perfect Bayesian equilibrium with $I > 0$.

9.2.1   Full Commitment

Full commitment allows the regulator to credibly specify both $R_1(q_1)$ and $R_2(q_2)$ to the firm prior to the first period.

The firm has four decision variables: q_1, q_2, I, and whether to produce in the second period, to produce in both periods or to produce only in the first period. The firm chooses to produce in the second period provided $\pi_1 < \pi_{12}$ where

$$\pi_1 = \max_{q_1, I} R_1(q_1) - c(q_1, I) - I$$

and

$$\pi_{12} = \max_{q_1, q_2, I} R_1(q_1) + R_2(q_2) - c(q_1, I) - c(q_2, I) - I.$$

Taking first order conditions we have that q_1^*, q_2^*, and I^* satisfy the following conditions

$$\frac{\partial R_1\left(q_1^*\right)}{\partial q_1} = \frac{\partial c\left(q_1^*, I^*\right)}{\partial q_1}$$

$$\frac{\partial R_2\left(q_2^*\right)}{\partial q_2} = \frac{\partial c\left(q_2^*, I^*\right)}{\partial q_2}$$

$$\frac{c\left(q_1^*, I^*\right)}{\partial I} = -1 \text{ if } \pi_1 > \pi_{12}$$

$$\frac{c\left(q_1^*, I^*\right)}{\partial I} + \frac{c\left(q_2^*, I^*\right)}{\partial I} = -1 \text{ if } \pi_1 \leq \pi_{12}.$$

Finally, the firm must also be willing to participate so: $\pi_1 \geq 0$ or $\pi_{12} \geq 0$.

Now we turn our attention to the regulator. The regulator solves

$$\max q_1 + q_2 - R_1\left(q_1\right) - R_2\left(q_2\right)$$

subject to the incentive constraints of the firm. We immediately see, taking first order conditions and substituting, that the optimum requires

$$q_1^* = q_2^*$$

$$\frac{c\left(q_2^*, I^*\right)}{\partial q_2} = \frac{c\left(q_1^*, I^*\right)}{\partial q_1} = 1$$

$$\frac{c\left(q_2^*, I^*\right)}{\partial I} = \frac{c\left(q_1^*, I^*\right)}{\partial I} = -\frac{1}{2}$$

$$\pi_{12} \geq \pi_1$$

$$\pi_{12} \geq 0.$$

This can be achieved under full commitment by the following contract

$$R_1\left(q_1\right) = q_1 - A_1; R_2\left(q_2\right) = q_2 - A_2$$

where

$$A_1 = q_1^* - c\left(q_1^*, I^*\right)$$

and

$$A_2 = q_2^* - c\left(q_2^*, I^*\right) - I^*.$$

The firm solves

$$\max_{q_1, q_2, I}\left\{q_1 - A_1 + q_2 - A_2 - c\left(q_1, I\right) - c\left(q_2, I\right) - I\right\}.$$

In equilibrium the regulator compensates the firm for its production costs in the first period and its production costs and investment costs in the second period such that the best the firm can do is $\pi_{12} = 0$.

9.2.2 No Commitment

Suppose this game has a pure strategy perfect Bayesian equilibrium denoted by $(q_1^*, q_2^*, I^*, R_1(q_1), R_2(q_2))$. First, in an equilibrium without commitment the regulator will offer to cover the firm's production costs in the second period, i.e., $\pi_2 = 0$, since the investment costs are at this point sunk and the firm will choose to produce in the second period. It is always possible and profitable for the regulator to do so given the form of the firm's cost function. Second, observe that the total payoff to the firm must be 0 in equilibrium. If $\pi_{12} > 0$ the regulator could simply reduce $R_1(q_1)$ by the amount of π_{12} in a lump sum manner improving its own payoff by π_{12} and not violating any of the incentive constraints of the firm. This implies that the payment made to the firm in the first period must be equal to the investment plus production costs $R_1(q_1^*) = c(q_1^*, I^*) + I^*$.

Given that the firm is producing in period 2 we know that

$$\frac{c(q_1^*, I^*)}{\partial I} + \frac{c(q_2^*, I^*)}{\partial I} = -1$$

$$\Rightarrow \quad \frac{c(q_1^*, I^*)}{\partial I} > -1$$

Using this, if $I^* > 0$ a profitable deviation for the firm is to reduce its investment I and not to produce in the second period since

$$\frac{\partial \pi_1(q_1^*, I^*)}{\partial I} = -1 - \frac{c(q_1^*, I^*)}{\partial I} < 0.$$

Therefore a pure strategy perfect Bayesian equilibrium cannot have $I^* > 0$.

9.3   Question 36

Consider the soft-budget constraint setting discussed in Chapter 9 (section 9.1.3), with the following variation: Assume each individual investor is infinitesimal, but can, in a first stage of the game, join a "small creditor," with one unit of funds in total, or a "large creditor," with two units of funds. Assume away agency problems between the manager running this undertaking and the small investors. Beyond this initial stage, the setting is as in section 9.1.3.

1. Assuming first a pure adverse selection setting for entrepreneurs (that is, the good entrepreneur can choose only a "quick" project), determine the equilibrium (assuming that creditors plagued by the soft budget constraint can never hope to get a higher probability of good entrepreneurs than the population average β–to get rid of "Rothschild-Stiglitz nonexistence problems" discussed in Chapter 13).

2. Add moral hazard for good entrepreneurs; that is, they can choose between the "quick" project and a "good but slow" project, whose payoffs are as

in section 9.1.3.3. When is there a single equilibrium of the game? When are there two (Pareto-ranked) equilibria?

9.3.1 Pure Adverse Selection

This question is based on Dewatripont & Maskin (1995).

In this exercise there are two types of entrepreneurs (good and bad), and the population prior of a good entrepreneurs is β. The profitability of a bad project depends on the monitoring effort level a to be exerted by the initial creditor. Specifically, we assume that the gross (discounted) financial return of a bad project is either 0 or $\overline{\pi}_B$ and the probability of $\overline{\pi}_B$ is a. Finally we assume that a is private information to the initial creditor, who incurs effort cost $\psi(a)$ which is increasing and convex in a.

In the case where the initial creditor is also the one refinancing a bad firm, it chooses an effort level a^* which fully internalizes the benefit of monitoring, that is

$$\pi_B^* \equiv \max_a \{a\overline{\pi}_B - \psi(a)\}$$

which implies $\overline{\pi}_B = \psi'(a^*)$. If the initial creditor is liquidity constrained, refinancing must come from a new creditor. Assuming also limited initial resources for the firm as well as the initial creditor, the new creditor has to be paid exclusively out of the return of the project. Define $\widehat{a}$ the expectation of monitoring effort a by the new creditor. Under perfect competition among new creditors, the refinancing contract will grant the new creditor $\frac{1}{\widehat{a}}$ in case the project is successful and generates $\overline{\pi}_B$. For a given $\widehat{a}$, the initial creditor will solve

$$\max_a \left\{ a \left[\overline{\pi}_B - \frac{1}{\widehat{a}}\right] - \psi(a) + 1 \right\} = \pi_B^{**}.$$

In equilibrium, the chosen effort level a^{**} is equal to $\widehat{a}$, and satisfies $\overline{\pi}_B = \psi'(a^{**}) + \frac{1}{a^{**}}$. Consequently, a^{**} is lower than a^*, and the associated continuation value of the project π_B^{**} is lower than π_B^*.

It is easy to see here that if $\pi_B^{**} < 1$ the size of the small creditor only allows it to finance an entrepreneur for one period such that it would be incapable of getting refinancing in the event that the project was bad. In other words it faces a hard budget constraint.

The large creditor has two units of funds to utilize in the first period and can afford to invest in up to two projects. The creditor is described as diversified if it invests in only one project and undiversified if it invests in two. If it only invests in one project in the first period it has a soft budget constraint because it will always have sufficient funds on hand in the second period to refinance a bad project. If it finances two projects, refinancing depends on the mix of projects in its portfolio. If both projects are bad then there will be no funds on hand after the first period to provide refinancing. If the other project is good then the funds from this project can be used to refinance the bad project after the first period.

Now to the question. In this question we assume that the creditor(s) that exist(s) in equilibrium will be the one(s) that can offer the investors the highest rate of return for their money. It is assumed that the creditors have all the bargaining power and can extract all the surplus from the entrepreneur.

Case 1: $\pi_B^{**} < 1$

In this case the small creditor has a hard budget constraint and so will only attract good entrepreneurs. It therefore generates a rate of return π_G. This is strictly greater than the rate of return the large creditor can generate since it has a soft budget constraint and will attract a proportion of bad entrepreneurs which necessarily will push the maximum rate of return it can achieve down.

Case 2: $\pi_B^{**} \geq 1$

Now both the small and large creditors have soft budget constraints and will attract a proportion of bad entrepreneurs. In this case the large creditor will be able to offer a higher rate of return because it fully internalizes the effects of monitoring in its choice of effort. Its choice is therefore more efficient and it generates a higher rate of return than the small creditor can do.

9.3.2   Adverse Selection & Moral Hazard

In this part of the question (if $\pi_B^{**} < 1 < \pi_B^*$) the small creditor may only attract good entrepreneurs wishing to undertake quick projects due to the hard budget constraint so it can offer a similar rate of return as earlier $R_S = \pi_G$. The large creditor on the other hand may also attract the good entrepreneurs with good but slow projects (denoted by v) because they can provide the additional funds for refinancing. Note that we assume the private benefit from undertaking a good but slow project E_v is greater than the private benefit of a good project $E_v \geq E_G$. If this is not the case then we are back in the case of part (1) and have a single equilibrium. We therefore assume $E_v \geq E_G$ for the rest of the question. Furthermore the entrepreneur receives private benefit E_t if a good but slow project is terminated after one period.

We assume that the choice of project type by the entrepreneur is made at the time of joining a creditor. A creditor's subsequent monitoring intensity depends on its period 1 beliefs about project quality. A large creditor expends effort $a^*(\tilde{a})$ such that $(1 - \tilde{a})\bar{\pi}_p = \psi'(a^*(\tilde{a}))$, where ψ is the cost of effort, $\tilde{a}$ is the probability the project is good but slow, and $1 - \tilde{a}$ is the probability it is poor. For large creditors with pessimistic beliefs ($\tilde{a} = 0$) define $a^*(0) = a^*$ which generates the return π^*. Similarly we can define $a^{**}(\tilde{a})$ for small creditors and $a^{**}(0) = a^{**}$ which generates return $R_S = \pi_B^{**}$.

Refinancing decisions also depend on $\tilde{a}$. Pessimistic beliefs (low values of $\tilde{a}$) lead to short-termism–the choice of good over very profitable projects–because good entrepreneurs believe that long-term projects will not be refinanced.

Single Equilibrium

If $\pi_G^{**} < 1$ then there exists an equilibrium in which only small creditors exist and only good projects are chosen. Suppose that creditors believe with a high probability that if a project is refinanced then it is poor. Good entrepreneurs that join a small fund will choose good projects because $\pi_G^{**} < 1$ and pessimistic beliefs on behalf of the creditor imply that there will be no refinancing for two period projects. This justifies the beliefs of the creditors.

This equilibrium can be highly inefficient if β is close to 1. If R_v is big and if β is close enough to 1 then it will be better from a social standpoint to put up with bad projects for the sake of the very good ones. Under some conditions there exists another more efficient equilibrium than the previous one.

Two Equilibria

Suppose $\pi_G^{**} < 1$, $E_v = E_G$, and $\beta R_v + (1-\beta)a^*(\beta)\overline{\pi}_p - \psi(a^*(\beta)) - 2 > R_g - 1$. Then there is another equilibrium where only big creditors exist and all good entrepreneurs select good but slow projects. This equilibrium Pareto dominates the previous equilibrium. Indeed, if investors all believe that entrepreneurs select good but slow projects then the large creditor can offer a rate of return greater than if all creditors chose good projects if

$$\beta R_v + (1-\beta)\pi_p^* - 2 > R_g - 1$$

which is just

$$\beta R_v + (1-\beta)a^*(\beta)\overline{R}_p - \psi(a^*(\beta)) - 2 > R_g - 1.$$

The intuition for this Pareto dominance is straightforward. The funder receives zero profits and so is indifferent. By revealed preference good entrepreneurs are better off since they could have gone to small funders. Bad entrepreneurs are better off since they are subsidized.

9.4 Question 37

Consider the following investment/insurance problem under private information: A risk-averse agent invests an amount $p/2$ in a project with random income shocks in two periods $t = 1, 2$, with

$$w_1 = \begin{cases} 1 & \text{with probability } p \\ 0 & \text{with probability } 1 - p \end{cases}$$

and $w_2 \in \{0, 1\}$, with

$$\begin{cases} \Pr(w_2 = 1 \mid w_1 = 1) = \gamma \leq p \\ \Pr(w_2 = 1 \mid w_1 = 0) = \mu \geq p \end{cases}$$

where $\gamma > 0.5$ and $p < 1$. The agent's utility function is time separable: $U(c_1; c_2) = u(c_1) + u(c_2)$ with $u(c)$ taking the following piecewise linear form:

$$u(c) = \left\{ \begin{array}{ll} \frac{1}{2} + \frac{1}{2}(c - \frac{1}{2}) & \text{for } c \geq \frac{1}{2} \\ c & \text{for } c < \frac{1}{2} \end{array} \right.$$

The agent can obtain insurance against the income shocks at actuarially fair rates at the beginning of every period.

1. Characterize the first-best optimal consumption allocation under the assumption that the agent cannot do any private saving.

2. Assuming that income shocks are private information, show that when only spot contracts are feasible, the agent cannot get any insurance.

3. Suppose that the agent can borrow from and lend to a bank at zero interest rate. Characterize the agent's optimal payoff under borrowing and lending.

4. When is insurance in the form of borrowing and lending an optimal contract?

Chapter 10

Dynamic Moral Hazard

10.1 Question 38

Consider a two-period principal-agent problem, where, in period 1, the agent chooses effort level a, which produces independently and identically distributed profit outcomes in each period, $q_1 \in \{q_L, q_H\}$ and $q_2 \in \{q_L, q_H\}$. The profit outcome q_H occurs with probability $p(a)$–a strictly increasing function of a–and the outcome q_L with probability $[1 - p(a)]$, with $1 > p(a) > 0$ for all $a \in [0, \bar{a}]$, where $\bar{a} < \infty$. The agent's utility function is $u(w) - a$, with $u' > 0 ; u'' < 0$. The agent can neither borrow nor save, so that she is forced to consume what she earns in each period. The principal is risk-neutral and can borrow or lend at zero interest rate.

1. Let $\{w_L, w_H, w_{LL}, w_{LH}, w_{HL}, w_{HH}\}$ denote the agent's profit-contingent compensation in periods 1 and 2. Show that the optimal contingent-compensation contract must satisfy the equation

$$\frac{1}{u'(w_i)} = \frac{p(a)}{u'(w_{iH})} + \frac{1 - p(a)}{u'(w_{iL})}, \text{ for } i = L, H$$

2. Using Jensen's inequality show that

$$w_i \leq p(a) w_{iH} + [1 - p(a)] w_{iL}, \text{ for } i = L, H$$

   under the optimal contract, when $1/u'$ is concave.

3. Suppose now that under the preceding optimal contract the agent is allowed to save and borrow at date 1 following the realization of q_1. Explain why she would want to save.

10.2 Question 39

A firm has assets in place and a new investment opportunity, and lives for three periods. In period $t = 0$, the firm's debt structure is chosen (that is, its level of short-term debt D_1 maturing at $t = 1$, and long-term debt D_2 due at $t = 2$). At $t = 1$, the assets in place yield a return C_1, and a new investment opportunity appears that requires an investment outlay I. At $t = 2$, the assets in place yield a further return C_2 and the new investment project generates a cash-flow C_N, if it has been undertaken at $t = 1$. At $t = 2$, the firm is liquidated and proceeds are distributed to investors. That is, outstanding debt claims are repaid, when feasible, and the residual proceeds are distributed to shareholders. The cash flows C_1 and C_2 are known at $t = 0$, but C_N remains uncertain until $t = 2$. Ex ante it is common knowledge that $C_N \in \{C_L, C_H\}$ with $C_H > I > C_L > 0$ and $\Pr[C_N = C_H] \equiv \gamma$.

The firm is run by a manager who decides whether or not to undertake the project at $t = 1$. The manager is an empire builder. She always chooses to undertake the project if he can. So, if there is sufficient financial slack at $t = 1$, the manager will invest. If this is not the case, the manager will turn to a new lender (bank) for a loan to fund the investment outlays. (Funds borrowed at $t = 1$ can also be used to repay D_1.) Debt raised at $t = 1$ is junior to all existing debt, but senior to equity. The debts D_1 and D_2 cannot be renegotiated. If the firm defaults at $t = 1$, there is a bankruptcy cost $k > 0$ and the firm is liquidated. (There are no bankruptcy costs if the firm defaults at $t = 2$). Finally, all agents are risk neutral, and the riskless rate of return is zero.

1. Suppose that $C_1 = D_1$. Does this assumption prevent the manager from undertaking projects with a negative net present value (NPV) at $t = 1$? That is, how much additional funding can the manager raise, and what projects will be undertaken?

2. Relax the assumption that $C_1 = D_1$. State the condition (as a function of D_1 and D_2) for the manager to be able to undertake the new project.

3. What are the optimal values of D_1 and D_2? What values of D_1 and D_2 ensure that the investment will be undertaken if and only if its NPV is positive? Explain the role of short-term debt in affecting managerial investment behavior.

4. Now assume that C_1 is a random variable independent of C_N and with the known probability distribution $C_1 \in \{C_1^L, C_1^H\}$ with $C_1^H > C_1^L$ and $\Pr[C_1 = C_1^H] \equiv \eta$. Assume also that all projects have a negative NPV and that $I > C_1^H - C_1^L$. What are the optimal values of D_1 and D_2?

5. Drop the assumption in part 4. that all projects have a negative NPV. Suppose instead that the uncertainty about C_N is resolved at $t = 1$. That is, at the time the investment is made, the return is known. Assume further that $C_H = 2I = 4C_L$. (C_1 continues to be a random variable.) Show that for $I > C_1^H - C_1^L$, it is optimal to set $D_1 = C_1^L$ and $D_2 > C_2$. Explain why risky long-term debt dominates risky short-term debt in this case.

6. Assume now that the opposite condition holds, that is $I < C_1^H - C_1^L$. Show that risky short-term debt is necessary to avoid overinvestment. What are the costs associated with avoiding overinvestment?

10.2.1 Debt Equals Cash Flow

The manager may still be able to undertake the project even if it has a negative net present value at $t = 1$ and current funds only cover the short term debt because at $t = 2$ the assets in place will yield a further C_2. The manager can borrow against the net present value of the firm which is the difference between C_2 and the debt repayment D_2 at $t = 2$ and the expected present value of the cash flows from the project itself. Specifically the maximum the manager can borrow is $C_2 - D_2 + \gamma C_H + (1 - \gamma) C_L$. Therefore projects will be undertaken if

$$I \leq C_2 - D_2 + \gamma C_H + (1 - \gamma) C_L.$$

10.2.2 Relaxing the Constraint

There are now two conditions which determine whether the manager can undertake the project. The first is the no-borrowing condition which–when it holds–prevents the manager from undertaking the project utilizing only funds available at $t = 1$, that is
$$I \leq C_1 - D_1.$$

The second is the borrowing condition from above which must now incorporate the difference between C_1 and D_1 as well. The borrowing condition for the manager to be able to undertake the project is

$$I \leq C_1 + C_2 - D_1 - D_2 + \gamma C_H + (1 - \gamma) C_L.$$

10.2.3 Optimal Values of Debt

D_1 and D_2 to Ensure Optimal Investment

If $C_1 + C_2 = D_1 + D_2$ the second condition reduces to $I \leq \gamma C_H + (1 - \gamma) C_L$, which says that the project is only undertaken if the net present value is non-negative. However we still need to worry about the no-borrowing condition because the manager may be able to undertake a negative net present value project without borrowing if there are sufficient funds at $t = 1$. This can be prevented by setting $D_1 \geq C_1$. Here the role of short term debt is to limit the funds available to the manager and force the manager to go to a bank in order to finance the project. By forcing the manager to go to the bank it creates a situation whereby the bank prevents the manager from undertaking any projects which do not have a positive net present value. The bank effectively monitors the manager's investment decisions so that only good investments are actually made despite the manager wanting to invest in every project.

10.2.4   Random First-Period Cash Flow

Optimal D_1 and D_2

Here we want to insure that there is no liquidation in period $t = 1$ (when there is a bankruptcy cost), liquidation in period $t = 2$, and that the project is not undertaken. Thus to ensure no liquidation in $t = 1$ we require

$$C_1 - D_1 \geq 0$$

and in order to ensure that the project is never undertaken, we require for any C_1

$$C_1 - D_1 \leq I$$

and

$$C_1 + C_2 - D_1 - D_2 + \gamma C_H + (1 - \gamma)C_L - I < 0.$$

The first condition requires

$$C_1^L \geq D_1$$

while the last equation requires

$$C_1^H + C_2 - D_1 + \gamma C_H + (1 - \gamma)C_L - I < D_2.$$

Thus we can set

$$C_1^L = D_1$$

and since

$$C_1^H - C_2^L < I$$

we only require that

$$C_1^H + C_2 - C_1^L + \gamma C_H + (1 - \gamma)C_L - I < D_2.$$

10.2.5   Known New Investment Return

As before

$$D_1 = C_1^L$$

to ensure that there is no liquidation in $t = 1$. Now we need

$$D_2 > C_2$$

to ensure that there is no overinvestment since we could have $C_N = C_L$ and $I - C_L > 0$ in which case the manager would still want to invest (inefficiently). He can do this if $C_1^i = C_1^H$ and $C_1^H - C_1^L + C_L > I$. Thus, to ensure this is not possible, we still need to have

$$C_1^H - C_1^L + C_L + (C_2 - D_2) < I$$

which requires $D_2 > C_2$. Here the risky–but senior–long term debt polices the incentive for overinvestment and does not incur the potential bankruptcy cost associated with risky short term debt.

10.2.6 Need for Short-Term Risky Debt

Here without liquidation in period $t = 1$ we would always have investment since it can be financed even without borrowing. Thus to avoid overinvestment we set D_1 such that the investment cannot be financed if it is inefficient. This necessarily requires $D_1 > C_1^L$ and thus we will have liquidation in period $t = 1$ when $C_1^i = C_1^L$. The costs associated with avoiding overinvestment are incurred when the firm is liquidated; they are the expected bankruptcy costs plus foregone period two cash flows from C_2 and potentially profitable investment projects.

10.3 Question 40

Consider a variant of Holmstrom's (1982a) career concern model: There are two identical periods. After the second period the manager retires. The output of the manager in period t is

$$q_t = \theta + a_t \varepsilon_t + (1 - a_t) e_t$$

where θ is the manager's unknown ability, $a_t \in [0, 1]$ is the manager's unobserved action, ε_t is an unobserved stochastic return term, and e_t is an observed stochastic return term. One may think of the manager's action as a decision to allocate a dollar between a firm-specific project, which returns ε_t, and a market project, which returns e_t. The allocation is known only to the manager.

The market pays the manager her expected value in each period $w_t = E[q_t|I_t]$, which depends on the market's information I_t and its expectation of the manager's action. Assume that the market's and the manager's first period beliefs about ability are such that θ is normally distributed with mean m_θ and precision (the inverse of the variance) h_θ. Beliefs in the second period are updated based on inferences about a_1, the observed outcome q_1, and the observed market return e_1.

Assume that the returns ε_t and e_t are independent across time as well as from one another. Each is normally distributed with zero mean and with precisions h_ε and h_e, respectively. The manager is strictly risk averse. Her preferences can be described by

$$u(w_1, w_2) = \sum_{t=1}^{2} (E[w_t] - \eta \operatorname{var}[w_t])$$

where w_t is her income in period t, E is the expectation operator, and var is the variance operator. The coefficient of risk aversion η is greater than 0. Note that there is no cost associated with choosing a_t. However, a_t is constrained to lie in the interval [0,1].

1. Write down the equations that characterize a rational-expectations (self-fulfilling) equilibrium for this model.

2. Show that in the rational-expectations equilibrium the manager will necessarily choose the first-period allocation $a_1 = 0$; that is, she will invest all the money in the market project.

3. Would this conclusion be altered if we instead assumed that the firm-specific project had an expected return $E(\varepsilon_t) = 1$? Discuss.

10.3.1 Characterization of Rational-Expectations Equilibrium

We assume that the market return e_1 is observed by both parties only at the beginning of the second period. The manager is paid his expected output in periods by the firm so that the wage schedule must satisfy

$$
\begin{aligned}
w_1 &= E\left[q_1|I_1\right] = E[q_1]\\
w_2 &= E\left[q_2|I_2\right] = E[q_2|q_1, e_1].
\end{aligned}
$$

Furthermore, the manager chooses actions to maximize utility

$$
(a_1, a_2) \in \arg\max_{(a_1, a_2)} \left\{ \sum_{t=1}^{2} \left(E[w_t] - \eta \text{var}[w_t] \right) \right\}.
$$

These equations characterize a rational-expectations equilibrium. They can be rewritten in the following way

$$
\begin{aligned}
w_1 &= m_\theta\\
w_2 &= E\left[\theta|q_1, e_1\right].
\end{aligned}
$$

Firms conjecture that managers choose action $\widehat{a}_1$ and $\widehat{a}_2$ in equilibrium. Thus, we have

$$
\begin{aligned}
w_2 &= E\left[\theta|e_1\right] + \frac{\text{cov}(\theta, q_1|e_1)}{\text{var}(q_1|e_1)} \{q_1 - E[q_1|e_1]\}\\[2mm]
&= m_\theta + \frac{\frac{1}{h_\theta}}{\frac{1}{h_\theta} + \frac{\widehat{a}_1^2}{h_\varepsilon}} \{\theta + a_1\varepsilon_1 + (1 - a_1)e_1 - [m_\theta + (1 - \widehat{a}_1)e_1]\}\\[2mm]
&= \frac{h_\theta m_\theta + \frac{h_\varepsilon}{\widehat{a}_1^2} [\theta + a_1\varepsilon_1 + (\widehat{a}_1 - a_1)e_1]}{h_\theta + \frac{h_\varepsilon}{\widehat{a}_1^2}}.
\end{aligned}
$$

Note that a_2 has no effect on the expected output and hence the wage in period 2. Hence, it is not pinned down and so we have $a_2 \in [0, 1]$. Furthermore, a_1 does not affect w_1 but does affect the variance of the signal needed to calculate wages in period 2. We now take expectations with respect to the manager's information at the start of period 1 and obtain

$$
\begin{aligned}
E(w_1) &= m_\theta \\
\mathrm{var}(w_1) &= 0 \\
E(w_2) &= \frac{h_\theta m_\theta + \frac{h_\varepsilon}{\widehat{a}_1^2} m_\theta}{h_\theta + \frac{h_\varepsilon}{\widehat{a}_1^2}} = m_\theta \\
\mathrm{var}(w_2) &= \left(\frac{\frac{h_\varepsilon}{\widehat{a}_1^2}}{h_\theta + \frac{h_\varepsilon}{\widehat{a}_1^2}}\right)^2 \left(\frac{1}{h_\theta} + \frac{a_1^2}{h_\varepsilon} + \frac{(\widehat{a}_1 - a_1)^2}{h_e}\right).
\end{aligned}
$$

Thus, the problem now reduces to

$$
\begin{aligned}
w_1 &= m_\theta \\
w_2 &= \frac{h_\theta m_\theta + \frac{h_\varepsilon}{\widehat{a}_1^2}\left[\theta + a_1 \varepsilon_1 + (\widehat{a}_1 - a_1)e_1\right]}{h_\theta + \frac{h_\varepsilon}{\widehat{a}_1^2}} \\
a_1 &\in \underset{a_1 \in [0,1]}{\arg\max}\left\{2m_\theta - \eta\left[\left(\frac{\frac{h_\varepsilon}{\widehat{a}_1^2}}{h_\theta + \frac{h_\varepsilon}{\widehat{a}_1^2}}\right)^2 \left(\frac{1}{h_\theta} + \frac{a_1^2}{h_\varepsilon} + \frac{(\widehat{a}_1 - a_1)^2}{h_e}\right)\right]\right\} \\
a_2 &\in [0,1]
\end{aligned}
$$

and $\widehat{a}_1 = a_1$ in equilibrium.

10.3.2 First-Period Allocation

Solving the manager's problem we obtain the following first order condition

$$
\frac{2a_1}{h_\varepsilon} - \frac{2(\widehat{a}_1 - a_1)}{h_e} = 0
$$

which can be simplified to

$$
a_1 = \frac{h_\varepsilon}{h_e + h_\varepsilon}\widehat{a}_1.
$$

In equilibrium $\widehat{a}_1 = a_1$, so it must be the case that $a_1 = 0$ as required since $\frac{h_\varepsilon}{h_e + h_\varepsilon} < 1$.

10.3.3 Positive Return of Firm-Specific Project

From our previous discussion we have

$$
\begin{aligned}
w_1 &= E\left[q_1 | I_1\right] \\
&= m_\theta + \widehat{a}_1
\end{aligned}
$$

where we substituted the market's conjecture $\widehat{a}_1$ for a_1 and used the fact that $E\left[\varepsilon_t\right] = 1$. Furthermore, the second-period wage is now

$$
\begin{aligned}
w_2 &= E\left[q_2 | I_2\right] \\
&= E\left[\theta | q_1, e_1\right] + \widehat{a}_2.
\end{aligned}
$$

Hence

$$
\begin{aligned}
w_2 &= E\left[\theta|q_1, e_1\right] + \frac{\text{cov}(\theta, q_1|e_1)}{\text{var}(q_1|e_1)}\{q_1 - E[q_1|e_1]\} + \widehat{a}_2 \\[2mm]
&= m_\theta + \frac{\frac{1}{h_\theta}}{\frac{1}{h_\theta} + \frac{\widehat{a}_1^2}{h_\varepsilon}}\{\theta + a_1\varepsilon_1 + (1 - a_1)e_1 - [m_\theta + \widehat{a}_1 + (1 - \widehat{a}_1)e_1]\} + \widehat{a}_2 \\[2mm]
&= \frac{h_\theta m_\theta + \frac{h_\varepsilon}{\widehat{a}_1^2}[\theta + a_1\varepsilon_1 - \widehat{a}_1 + (\widehat{a}_1 - a_1)e_1]}{h_\theta + \frac{h_\varepsilon}{\widehat{a}_1^2}} + \widehat{a}_2.
\end{aligned}
$$

Now, the wage payments for the manager are such that

$$
\begin{aligned}
E(w_1) &= m_\theta + \widehat{a}_1 \\[1mm]
\text{var}(w_1) &= 0 \\[1mm]
E(w_2) &= \frac{h_\theta m_\theta + \frac{h_\varepsilon}{\widehat{a}_1^2}[m_\theta + (a_1 - \widehat{a}_1)]}{h_\theta + \frac{h_\varepsilon}{\widehat{a}_1^2}} + \widehat{a}_2 \\[2mm]
&= m_\theta + \frac{\frac{h_\varepsilon}{\widehat{a}_1^2}}{h_\theta + \frac{h_\varepsilon}{\widehat{a}_1^2}}(a_1 - \widehat{a}_1) + \widehat{a}_2 \\[2mm]
\text{var}(w_2) &= \left(\frac{\frac{h_\varepsilon}{\widehat{a}_1^2}}{h_\theta + \frac{h_\varepsilon}{\widehat{a}_1^2}}\right)^2\left(\frac{1}{h_\theta} + \frac{a_1^2}{h_\varepsilon} + \frac{(\widehat{a}_1 - a_1)^2}{h_e}\right).
\end{aligned}
$$

Using these expressions we can again rewrite the manager's problem as

$$
a_1 \in \arg\max_{a_1 \in [0,1]} 2m_\theta + \widehat{a}_1 + \widehat{a}_2 + \frac{\frac{h_\varepsilon}{\widehat{a}_1^2}}{h_\theta + \frac{h_\varepsilon}{\widehat{a}_1^2}}(a_1 - \widehat{a}_1)
$$

$$
- \eta\left[\left(\frac{\frac{h_\varepsilon}{\widehat{a}_1^2}}{h_\theta + \frac{h_\varepsilon}{\widehat{a}_1^2}}\right)^2\left(\frac{1}{h_\theta} + \frac{a_1^2}{h_\varepsilon} + \frac{(\widehat{a}_1 - a_1)^2}{h_e}\right)\right]
$$

$$
a_2 \in [0, 1].
$$

The first order conditions with respect to a_1 yield

$$
\frac{\frac{h_\varepsilon}{\widehat{a}_1^2}}{h_\theta + \frac{h_\varepsilon}{\widehat{a}_1^2}} - \eta\left(\frac{\frac{h_\varepsilon}{\widehat{a}_1^2}}{h_\theta + \frac{h_\varepsilon}{\widehat{a}_1^2}}\right)^2\left(\frac{2a_1}{h_\varepsilon} - \frac{2(\widehat{a}_1 - a_1)}{h_e}\right) = 0.
$$

Noting that in a rational-expectations equilibrium $\widehat{a}_1 = a_1$ we have

$$
a_1 = \frac{a_1^2 h_\theta + h_\varepsilon}{2\eta}.
$$

Solving the resulting quadratic equation we obtain

$$
a_1 = \frac{\eta \pm \sqrt{\eta^2 - h_\theta h_\varepsilon}}{h_\theta} > 0.
$$

Note that there may be one or two solutions since $a_1 \leq 1$. The solution is unique if both roots are larger than 1. Otherwise, there are always two solutions.

Discussion

In this model a_1 has similar effects as in the original Holmstrom (1982a) model in that it allows the manager to influence the market's belief about his ability. In the first part where $E[\varepsilon_t] = 0$ the expected marginal benefit of dedicating resources to the unobservable firm-specific project is 0. Furthermore, in contrast to the market return e_t, the return of the firm-specific project ε_t is unobservable, and hence allocating resources to the firm-specific project only increases wage variability which hurts the risk-averse manager. Hence, $a_1 = 0$ in the first part of the model.

On the other hand when $E[\varepsilon_t] > 0$ the manager's expected marginal benefit of the firm-specific project is positive as it allows him to effectively influence the market's inference process about his ability (even though in equilibrium the market is not fooled). Thus, by allocating a strictly positive amount of resources to the firm-specific project the manager trades off the benefits of effectively influencing the market's inference process with the negative effects of increased wage risk.

Finally, note that this model also generates a "herding" conclusion. Rather than investing in a (superior) firm-specific project the manager might invest most (though not all of his resources) in an inferior market project with a return that is ex post observable to everyone.

Chapter 11

Incomplete Contracts

11.1 Question 41

An upstream supplier invests x dollars in period $t = 0$ in acquiring technical skills to produce customized software in period $t = 1$ for a downstream producer. The type of software required and the terms of trade can only be specified in period $t = 1$. The total surplus from trading the software in period $t = 1$ is given by $v(x)$, where $v(\cdot)$ is a strictly increasing, strictly concave function with $v'(0) > 1$, which is bounded above $[v(x) \to M < +\infty$ as $x \to +\infty]$. In period $t = 1$ the upstream and downstream producers are locked in a bilateral bargaining situation, resulting in an efficient trade and in a 50/50 split of the surplus from trade.

1. Explain why ex post spot contracting results in ex ante underinvestment.

2. Suppose now that a new computer to run the software is also available in period $t = 1$. With this new computer, total ex post surplus generated by the software increases from $v(x)$ to $V(x) = f[v(x)] > v(x)$, where $f' \geq 0$ and $f'' \leq 0$. What is the first-best level of investment in skills in period $t = 0$ given that the contracting parties have access to this new computer in period $t = 1$? Is this first-best investment level always higher than the first-best level of investment obtained when access to the new computer is denied?

3. Suppose now that the new computer can be owned either by (a) the upstream producer, (b) the downstream buyer, or (c) a third party owner. Under up- or downstream ownership there will be bilateral ex post bargaining resulting in a 50/50 split of the total surplus. Under third-party ownership of the new computer, there is trilateral ex post bargaining, and the owner of the computer gets the full marginal contribution of the computer, $V(x) - v(x)$, while the other two parties split the surplus $v(x)$ in half. Show that up- or downstream ownership dominates third-party ownership if $f' > 1$, but third-party-ownership dominates when $\frac{1}{2} < f' < 1$.

4. Explain why either upstream, downstream, or third-party ownership may dominate when $f' < \frac{1}{2}$.

5. How would your answers to parts 3. and 4. change if the trilateral bargaining solution were given by the Shapley value?

11.2   Question 42

Consider the following vertical integration problem: There are two risk-neutral managers, each running an asset a_i where $i = 1, 2$. Both managers make ex ante investments. Only ex post spot contracts regulating trade are feasible. Ex post trade at price P results in the following payoffs: $R(x_1) - P$ for manager 1 and $P - C(x_2)$ for manager 2, where the x_i's denote ex ante investment levels.

If the two managers do not trade with each other their respective payoffs are

$$r(x_1, A_1) - P_m \quad \text{and} \quad P_m - c(x_2, A_2)$$

where A_i denotes the collection of assets owned by manager i. In this problem, $A_i = \emptyset$ under j-integration, $A_i = \{a_1; a_2\}$ under i-integration, and $A_i = \{a_i\}$ under nonintegration.

As in the Grossman-Hart-Moore setting, it is assumed that

$$R(x_1) - C(x_2) > r(x_1, A_1) - c(x_2, A_2)$$

for all $(x_1, x_2) \in [0, \overline{x}]^2$ and all A_i,

$$R'(x_1) > r'(x_1, \{a_1, a_2\}) \geq r'(x_1, \{a_i\}) \geq r'(x_1, \emptyset) \geq 0$$

and

$$-C'(x_2) > -c'(x_2, \{a_1, a_2\}) \geq -c'(x_2, \{a_i\}) \geq -c'(x_2, \emptyset) \geq 0$$

1. Characterize the first-best allocation of assets and investment levels.

2. Assuming that the managers split the ex post gains from trade in half, identify conditions on $r'(x_i, A_i)$ and $c'(x_i, A_i)$ such that nonintegration is optimal.

3. Under the same assumption on ex post bargaining, identify conditions on $r'(x_i, A_i)$ and $c'(x_i, A_i)$ such that integration under the ownership of manager 1 is optimal.

4. Suppose now that

$$r(x_1, A_1) - P_m < \frac{R(x_1) - C(x_2)}{2}$$

for all $x_1 \in [0, \overline{x}]$ and all A_1. Suppose also that:

$$P_m - c(x_2, A_2) > \frac{R(x_1) - C(x_2)}{2}$$

for all $x_2 \in [0, \overline{x}]$ and all A_2. Under these assumptions, bargaining under an outside option would give the following outcome:

Equilibrium payoff of manager 1: $R(x_1) - C(x_1) - [P_m - c(x_2, A_2)]$
Equilibrium payoff of manager 2: $[P_m - c(x_2, A_2)]$

[The equilibrium payoff of manager 1 should be $R(x_1) - C(x_2) - [P_m - c(x_2, A_2)]$. –CCES]. In other words, manager 2 gets her outside option. In what way would the analysis and results about optimal ownership allocations and equilibrium investment levels change under this new bargaining solution?

11.2.1 First-Best Allocation of Assets and Investment Levels

To obtain meaningful interior solutions we assume that the benefits $R(x_1)$, $r(x_1, A_1)$, $-C(x_2)$, and $-c(x_2, A_2)$ are gross of linear investment costs and concave in x. For this question we make the same assumption as in Hart & Moore (1990), and section 11.2.1.3. The first-best allocation must maximize the total ex ante net benefits of the two managers under trade since

$$R(x_1) - C(x_2) - x_1 - x_2 > r(x_1, A_1) - c(x_2, A_2) - x_1 - x_2$$

for all $(x_1, x_2) \in [0, \overline{x}]^2$ and all A_i. Hence, the first-best solution $x^* = (x_1^*, x_2^*)$ is characterized by the following conditions:

$$\begin{aligned} R'(x_1^*) &= 1 \\ -C'(x_2^*) &= 1. \end{aligned}$$

The allocation of assets in this case is irrelevant since the expressions $R(x_1)$ and $C(x_2)$ are independent of the asset allocation.

11.2.2 Optimal Asset Ownership

Nonintegration

The surplus under nonintegration when no trade takes place is given by

$$r(x_1, \{a_1\}) - c(x_2, \{a_2\}).$$

As before the surplus from trade is $R(x_1) - C(x_2)$. The managers split the ex post surplus gain in half. The managers solve

$$\max_{x_1} r(x_1, \{a_1\}) - P_m$$

$$+ \frac{1}{2}[R(x_1) - C(x_2) - r(x_1, \{a_1\}) + c(x_2, \{a_2\})] - x_1$$

and

$$\max_{x_2} P_m - c(x_2, \{a_2\})$$

$$+ \frac{1}{2} \left[R(x_1) - C(x_2) - r(x_1, \{a_1\}) + c(x_2, \{a_2\}) \right] - x_2.$$

Thus the first order conditions that characterize the optimal investment levels $x^{no} = (x_1^{no}, x_2^{no})$ are

$$\begin{aligned} R'(x_1^{no}) + r'(x_1^{no}, \{a_1\}) &= 2 \\ -C'(x_2^{no}) - c'(x_2^{no}, \{a_2\}) &= 2. \end{aligned}$$

1-Integration

The surplus under 1-integration when trade does not take place is

$$r(x_1, \{a_1, a_2\}) - c(x_2, \{\emptyset\}).$$

Hence the managers solve

$$\max_{x_1} r(x_1, \{a_1, a_2\}) - P_m$$

$$+ \frac{1}{2} \left[R(x_1) - C(x_2) - r(x_1, \{a_1, a_2\}) + c(x_2, \{\emptyset\}) \right] - x_1$$

and

$$\max_{x_2} P_m - c(x_2, \{\emptyset\})$$

$$+ \frac{1}{2} \left[R(x_1) - C(x_2) - r(x_1, \{a_1, a_2\}) + c(x_2, \{\emptyset\}) \right] - x_2.$$

The first order conditions are

$$\begin{aligned} R'(x_1^{1-int}) + r'(x_1^{1-int}, \{a_1, a_2\}) &= 2 \\ -C'(x_2^{1-int}) - c'(x_2^{1-int}, \{\emptyset\}) &= 2. \end{aligned}$$

2-Integration

The no-trade surplus under 2-integration is

$$r(x_1, \{\emptyset\}) - c(x_2, \{a_1, a_2\})$$

so the managers solve

$$\max_{x_1} r(x_1, \{\emptyset\}) - P_m$$

$$+ \frac{1}{2} \left[R(x_1) - C(x_2) - r(x_1, \{\emptyset\}) + c(x_2, \{a_1, a_2\}) \right] - x_1$$

and

$$\max_{x_2} P_m - c(x_2, \{a_1, a_2\})$$

$$+ \frac{1}{2} \left[R\left(x_1\right) - C\left(x_2\right) - r(x_1, \{\emptyset\}) + c(x_2, \{a_1, a_2\}) \right] - x_2.$$

The resulting first order conditions can be rewritten as

$$R'(x_1^{2-int}) + r'(x_1^{2-int}, \{\emptyset\}) = 2$$
$$-C'(x_2^{2-int}) - c'(x_2^{2-int}, \{a_1, a_2\}) = 2.$$

11.2.3 Comparison

Using the first order conditions under the different ownership structures we can compare the resulting investment levels. Using the fact that

$$R'(x_1) > r'(x_1, \{a_1, a_2\}) \geq r'(x_1, \{a_i\}) \geq r'(x_1, \{\emptyset\}) \geq 0$$

and

$$-C'(x_2) > -c'(x_2, \{a_1, a_2\}) \geq -c'(x_2, \{a_i\}) \geq -c'(x_2, \{\emptyset\}) \geq 0$$

as well as the concavity of $R(x_1)$, $r(x_1, A_1)$, $-C(x_2)$, and $-c(x_2, A_2)$ we can establish the relationship

$$x_1^* > x_1^{1-int} \geq x_1^{no} \geq x_1^{2-int}$$
$$x_2^* > x_2^{2-int} \geq x_2^{no} \geq x_2^{1-int}.$$

Thus, under 1-integration manager 1 has optimal investment incentives and manager 2 has optimal incentives under 2-integration.

Sufficient conditions for nonintegration to be optimal are

$$r'(x_1, \{a_1\}) = r'(x_1, \{a_1, a_2\}) \Rightarrow x_1^{no} = x_1^{1-int}$$
$$c'(x_2, \{a_2\}) = c'(x_2, \{a_1, a_2\}) \Rightarrow x_2^{no} = x_2^{2-int}.$$

Nonintegration is optimal when we have independence.

From the above characterization of investment levels we can see that 1-integration gives manager 1 optimal incentives. Hence, a sufficient condition for 1-integration to be optimal is

$$c'(x_2, \{\emptyset\}) = c'(x_2, \{a_1, a_2\}) \Rightarrow x_2^{1-int} = x_2^{2-int}.$$

1-integration is optimal when the human capital of manager 1 is essential.

11.2.4 Ex Post Bargaining with an Outside Option

In the question $C(x_1)$ should be replaced by $C(x_2)$. Ex ante the managers now maximize the following payoffs

$$\max_{x_1} R(x_1) - C(x_2) - [P_m - c(x_2, A_2)] - x_1$$
$$\max_{x_2} P_m - c(x_2, A_2) - x_2.$$

Nonintegration

Under nonintegration the optimal ex ante investment levels are characterized by the following conditions

$$R'(x_1^{no}) = 1$$
$$-c'(x_2^{no}, \{a_2\}) = 1.$$

1-Integration

When both assets are owned by manager 1 the optimal investment levels are

$$R'(x_1^{1-int}) = 1$$
$$-c'(x_2^{1-int}, \{\emptyset\}) = 1.$$

2-Integration

Finally, when manager 2 owns both assets the investment levels are

$$R'(x_1^{2-int}) = 1$$
$$-c'(x_2^{2-int}, \{a_1, a_2\}) = 1.$$

Comparison

Looking at the first order conditions for manager 1 across the different ownership structures we immediately see that

$$x_1^* = x_1^{1-int} = x_1^{no} = x_1^{2-int}.$$

However, the optimal ex ante investment levels of manager 2 vary across the different regimes

$$x_2^* > x_2^{2-int} \geq x_2^{no} \geq x_2^{1-int}.$$

Hence the optimal ownership structure when the ex post bargaining process leaves only an outside option to manager 2 is 2-integration.

11.3   Question 43

Consider a firm seeking outside finance. At date 0, the firm needs to raise I and has no liquid funds. At date 1, it will have (verifiable) assets in place worth A and generate liquid returns C_1 that are assumed to be non-verifiable by outsiders (for example, because they are private information to the firm). We have $C_1 = C_1^H$ with probability β and $C_1 = 0$ with probability $1 - \beta$, where $\beta C_1^H \geq I$. The firm does not know the realization of C_1 at date 0. At date 2 the firm also has long-term returns (future earnings prospects) C_2, which are also unverifiable. The realization of C_2 will be known to the firm already at date 1. We have $C_2 = C_2^H$ with probability γ and $C_2 = C_2^L$ with probability $1 - \gamma$, $C_2^H > C_2^L > A$.

A contract between the firm and an outside investor is a pair of functions (P, L), where $P = P(\theta)$ and $L = L(\theta)$ depend on the information $\theta = (C_1, C_2)$ available at date 1. $P \leq C_1$ is the firm's payment made out of C_1, and $L \leq A$ is the firm's payment made by liquidating assets. If an amount L of assets is liquidated, long-term earnings to the firm will be $(1 - L/A)C_2$.

The firm and outside investors are risk neutral. At date 0, outside investors have costs of funds equal to one and offer competing investment contracts. The firm then chooses the most preferred one (randomizing if offers are identical), and this contract is executed. Formally, therefore at date 1 the firm announces its information, and the payments specified in the contract are carried out.

1. Write down the parties' utility functions and the contracting problem at date 0.

2. What is the first-best allocation?

3. Show that in the (second-best) optimal contracting problem the functions P and L must be monotone in C_2. Interpret.

4. Solve the contracting problem and discuss.

5. Now suppose that the parties will renegotiate date-1 inefficiencies whenever possible, that is, whenever the firm has the funds to compensate the investor for not liquidating. Suppose also, to simplify matters, that information is symmetric ex post, that is, that the investor observes θ (but that θ is still nonverifiable). Suppppose finally that in these renegotiations the firm has all the bargaining power (that is, makes a take-it-or-leave-it offer to the investor). Determine the optimal renegotiation-proof contract.

6. Compare your results in part 5 to those in part 4.

11.4   Question 44

An entrepreneur with no initial wealth has a project which requires an initial investment K and whose output can take two values: $q \in \{0, 1\}$. The market interest rate is normalized to zero. The entrepreneur offers a financial contract to an investor. After the initial investment, both parties observe the realization of the state of the world, $\theta \in \{B, G\}$, which, however, is not observable by a court and thus not contractable. Instead, a contract can be contingent on the realization of a binary signal, s, which is verifiable in a court. The signal is distributed as follows: If $\theta = G$, $s = 1$ with probability one. If $\theta = B$, then $s = 1$ with probability γ and $s = 0$ with probability $1 - \gamma$. Assume γ is sufficiently small but strictly positive.

In each state of the world, an action a has to be taken: $a \in \{S, C\}$, where S is interpreted as "stop" (downsize, liquidate), and C is interpreted as "continue." The probability of high output depends on the realized state of the world and on the action chosen: $\Pr[q = 1 | \theta, a] = a_\theta$. (Note that a_θ also expresses the expected monetary return of the project given action a and state θ.) While the investor cares only about monetary returns, the entrepreneur also has a private nonmonetary benefit h from choosing C rather than S. Monetary and nonmonetary returns satisfy the following inequalities:

$$
\begin{aligned}
C_G &< S_G < C_G + h \\
C_B + h &< S_B \\
S_G - C_G &< S_B - C_B
\end{aligned}
$$

Actions cannot be described in an ex ante contract. Instead, a contract specifies control rights, that is, it specifies which party has the right to choose the action. Besides, the contract specifies the entrepreneur's compensation as a function of the realized s and q. If the party in control chooses an action that is not Pareto optimal, the parties can try and renegotiate to an optimal outcome. Assume that the entrepreneur has all the bargaining power in renegotiation.

1. For each of the following control structures, find the values of K for which a contract implementing the first-best action choice is feasible: (a) entrepreneurial control; (b) investor control; (c) contingent control (E has control when $s = 1$, I has control when $s = 0$ [E and I refer to the entrepreneur and investor respectively. –CCES]).

2. Under what conditions does each control structure dominate?

3. Compare your results with Proposition 5 in Aghion & Bolton (1992).

11.4.1   Feasibility Constraints

We assume that $h > 0$. We first analyze the inequalities given in the question to determine the efficient actions in the two states of nature. Since

$$
S_G < C_G + h
$$

it is efficient to continue in the good state. However, in the bad state we have

$$
C_B + h < S_B
$$

and so liquidation is efficient.

Entrepreneurial Control

Under entrepreneurial control, actions are chosen to maximize the entrepreneur's payoff

$$
a_\theta^E = \arg\max_a \{\Pr(q = 1 | a, \theta) - t(s, \theta) + h(a)\}
$$

where $t(s, q)$ is the repayment for a signal s and a return q. Note that because of the binary structure of the problem we can rewrite the repayment transfer as

$$
t(s, q) = t_s q + k_s \leq q.
$$

We can therefore rewrite the entrepreneur's optimal action as

$$a_\theta^E = \arg\max_a \{\Pr(q|a,\theta)(1-t_s) - k_s + h(a)\}.$$

Since the investor has unlimited wealth he can always bribe the entrepreneur to take the ex post efficient action.

Clearly, because of the private benefits h the entrepreneur is biased towards continuation and so the efficient action and the preferred action of the entrepreneur coincide in the good state. The investor and entrepreneur have three possible contractual strategies to ensure that the entrepreneur chooses liquidation over continuation in the bad state.

Full Ex Post renegotiation The parties can rely entirely on ex post renegotiation. The contract that provides the highest return to the investor sets $t_s = 1$ and $k_s = 0$ for $s = 0, 1$. With this contract the entrepreneur's choice would be entirely determined by her private benefits and she would choose to continue irrespective of the state. However, in the bad state she will give the investor an offer that makes the latter indifferent between continuation and liquidation while ensuring a higher payoff for the entrepreneur. The investor's ex ante expected payoff is then

$$\Pi_R = pC_G + (1-p)C_B$$

where $p = \Pr(\theta = G)$.

Renegotiation-Proof contract The parties can also write a renegotiation-proof contract that induces the entrepreneur to choose liquidation over continuation in the bad state, yields the highest return to the investor and ensures that the parties have no incentive to renegotiate the initial contract. The entrepreneur's incentive compatibility constraint in the bad state for a given signal s is

$$S_B(1-t_s) - k_s \geq C_B(1-t_s) - k_s + h.$$

Thus, t_s is set at the highest possible value that still satisfies the above constraint so that we obtain

$$t_s = \frac{S_B - C_B - h}{S_B - C_B}$$

for $s = 0, 1$. Furthermore, from the entrepreneur's wealth constraint we know that

$$t_s q + k_s \leq q$$

in particular for $q = 0$

$$k_s \leq 0.$$

Clearly, to maximize the investor's expected payoff we set $k_s = 0$. Under the best renegotiation-proof contract for the investor, he is expected to receive

$$
\begin{aligned}
\Pi_{NR} &= p(C_G t_s + k_s) + (1-p)(S_B t_s + k_s) \\
&= [pC_G + (1-p) S_B] t_s \\
&= [pC_G + (1-p) S_B] \frac{S_B - C_B - h}{S_B - C_B}.
\end{aligned}
$$

Partial Renegotiation   Finally, the parties could also write a contract that is partially renegotiation-proof when $s = 0$. That is to say, the incentive compatibility constraint holds in the bad state, so that

$$
t_0 = \frac{S_B - C_B - h}{S_B - C_B}.
$$

Yet, there is renegotiation in equilibrium when $s = 1$ and so the repayment share is set so that

$$
t_1 = 1.
$$

Hence, without further renegotiation in the bad state the entrepreneur would choose to continue when $s = 1$ and to liquidate when $s = 0$. To ensure the maximum return for the investor, both fixed payments are set equal to zero, $k_s = 0$. The investor therefore receives

$$
\begin{aligned}
\Pi_{PR} = \Pr(s = 1, \theta = G)C_G t_1 + \Pr(s = 0, \theta = G)C_G t_0 \\
+ \Pr(s = 1, \theta = B)C_B t_1 + \Pr(s = 0, \theta = B)S_B t_0
\end{aligned}
$$

which simplifies to

$$
\begin{aligned}
\Pi_{PR} &= pC_G t_1 + (1-p)\gamma C_B t_1 + (1-p)(1-\gamma)S_B t_0 \\
&= pC_G + (1-p)\left[\gamma C_B + (1-\gamma)S_B \frac{S_B - C_B - h}{S_B - C_B}\right].
\end{aligned}
$$

Note that the investor only receives C_B in the bad state when $s = 1$ since all the bargaining power rests with the entrepreneur.

Comparison   As a result, entrepreneurial control is feasible if and only if

$$
\max \{\Pi_R, \Pi_{NR}, \Pi_{PR}\} \geq K.
$$

Investor Control

The investor's ex post payoff is

$$
\Pr(q = 1 | a, \theta)t_s + k_s
$$

so the investor will maximize monetary payoffs when $t_s \geq 0$. We can restrict attention to $t_s \geq 0$ under investor control. In such a case, without renegotiation the investor will inefficiently choose to liquidate irrespective of the state since

$$C_G < S_G$$
$$C_B < S_B.$$

Moreover, renegotiation no longer ensures that the efficient action is implemented in the good state since the entrepreneur is wealth-constrained. The entrepreneur is only able to effectively bribe the investor when her total pledgeable wealth in the good state under the renegotiated action (that is, to continue rather than to shut down) is at least as large as the minimum bribe required to persuade the investor to continue rather than liquidate. Thus, ex post efficiency is assured if and only if

$$C_G(1 - t_s) - k_s \geq t_s S_G - t_s C_G.$$

Rewriting this condition, we obtain

$$t_s \leq \frac{C_G - k_s}{S_G}.$$

Setting $t_s = \frac{C_G - k_s}{S_G}$ the investor's ex ante expected payoff is given by

$$
\begin{aligned}
\Pi_I &= pC_G + (1 - p)\left\{\gamma\left[S_B t_1 + k_1\right] + (1 - \gamma)\left[S_B t_0 + k_0\right]\right\} \\
&= pC_G + (1 - p)\left\{\gamma\left[S_B\frac{C_G - k_1}{S_G} + k_1\right] + (1 - \gamma)\left[S_B\frac{C_G - k_0}{S_G} + k_0\right]\right\}.
\end{aligned}
$$

But assuming that $S_B < S_G$ the investor's profit is strictly increasing in k_1 and k_0 so that they will be set at their maximum value, i.e., equal to zero. Under investor control $t_0 = 1$ since $\Pr(s = 0|\theta = G) = 0$, and thus this does not create an inefficiency. Consequently, we have

$$
\begin{aligned}
\Pi_I &= pC_G + (1 - p)\left[\gamma\frac{C_G}{S_G}S_B + (1 - \gamma)S_B\right] \\
\pi_I &= ph + (1 - p)\left[\gamma\left(1 - \frac{C_G}{S_G}\right)S_B\right]
\end{aligned}
$$

and investor control is efficient and feasible if and only if

$$\Pi_I \geq K.$$

Contingent Control

In the present setting the investor is always biased towards liquidation whereas the entrepreneur always favors continuation. A signal-contingent allocation that gives control to the entrepreneur if $s = 1$ and gives control to the investor if $s = 0$ may therefore be a viable choice. Suppose that

$$
\begin{aligned}
t_s &= 1 \\
k_s &= 0
\end{aligned}
$$

for $s = 0, 1$ which gives the maximum payoff to the investor. Under these circumstances without renegotiation the entrepreneur will always continue the project when he is in control, whereas the investor will always shut it down. Although this arrangement implements the efficient actions when $(s, \theta) = (1, G)$ and $(s, \theta) = (0, B)$, it could potentially create an inefficiency in the case $(s, \theta) = (1, B)$ and $(s, \theta) = (0, G)$. However, renegotiation ensures that the entrepreneur will liquidate when $(s, \theta) = (1, B)$. In that case, the entrepreneur extracts all the surplus from renegotiation and obtains $S_B - C_B$ whereas the investor receives C_B. Due to the entrepreneur's wealth constraint the efficient choice to continue would not be implemented when $(s, \theta) = (0, G)$, yet in our case since $\Pr(s = 0 | \theta = B) = 0$ this case can never occur. As a result the first best actions are implemented and the parties' payoffs are given by

$$
\begin{aligned}
\Pi_{SC} &= pC_G + (1 - p) \left[\gamma C_B + (1 - \gamma) S_B \right] \\
\pi_{SC} &= ph + (1 - p)\gamma \left(S_B - C_B \right).
\end{aligned}
$$

As a result, contingent control that implements the first best is feasible if and only if

$$
\Pi_{SC} \geq K.
$$

11.4.2 Optimal Control Structures

We now compare the investor's payoffs obtained under the different structures. First, note that

$$
\Pi_{SC} > \Pi_{PR}
$$

since $\frac{S_B - C_B - h}{S_B - C_B} < 1$. Second, we have

$$
\Pi_{SC} > \Pi_R
$$

since $S_B > C_B$. Third, we can see that

$$
\Pi_{SC} > \Pi_{NR}
$$

if and only if γ is sufficiently low, in particular,

$$
\gamma < \frac{(1 - t) \left[pC_G + (1 - p) S_B \right]}{(1 - p) \left(S_B - C_B \right)} \equiv \gamma_{SC}.
$$

where $t = \frac{S_B - C_B - h}{S_B - C_B}$. Thus, signal-contingent control only dominates entrepreneur control with renegotiation-proof contracts if the signal is sufficiently informative.

Now, let us compare signal-contingent control with investor control using signal-contingent repayments. Clearly, we have

$$\Pi_{SC} > \widehat{\Pi}_I$$

if and only if

$$\frac{C_B}{S_B} > \frac{C_G}{S_G}.$$

That is, contingent control dominates investor control whenever the ratio of monetary returns of continuation and liquidation is lower in the good state than in the bad state.

Let us also compare investor control with entrepreneur control when investor control dominates signal-contingent control, that is when $\frac{C_B}{S_B} < \frac{C_G}{S_G}$. Obviously, since $\Pi_{SC} > \max\{\Pi_R, \Pi_{PR}\}$ and $\widehat{\Pi}_I > \Pi_{SC}$ when $\frac{C_B}{S_B} < \frac{C_G}{S_G}$ it must always be the case that

$$\widehat{\Pi}_I > \Pi_R.$$

We can verify that this condition holds when

$$\gamma < \frac{(S_B - C_B)\, S_G}{(S_G - C_G)\, S_B}$$

but $\frac{C_B}{S_B} < \frac{C_G}{S_G}$, $\frac{(S_B - C_B)S_G}{(S_G - C_G)S_B} > 1$ and so this condition is always satisfied. Similarly,

$$\widehat{\Pi}_I > \Pi_{PR}$$

$\Leftrightarrow$

$$\frac{\gamma}{1 - \gamma} > -\frac{S_B(1 - t)}{\frac{C_G}{S_G} S_B - C_B}.$$

Again this condition is always satisfied since

$$-\frac{S_B(1 - t)}{\frac{C_G}{S_G} S_B - C_B} < 0.$$

Lastly, we have

$$\widehat{\Pi}_I > \Pi_{NR}$$

if and only if

$$\gamma < \frac{(1 - t)\,[pC_G + (1 - p)\, S_B]}{(1 - p)\, \frac{S_B}{S_G}\, (S_G - C_G)} \equiv \gamma_I.$$

Clearly, we have

$$\gamma_I > \gamma_{SC}$$

if and only if

$$\frac{C_B}{S_B} < \frac{C_G}{S_G}.$$

Note also that we have

$$\pi_{SC} > \widehat{\pi}_I$$

if and only if

$$\frac{C_B}{S_B} < \frac{C_G}{S_G}.$$

Thus, when this condition holds, the entrepreneur prefers signal-contingent control.

In summary, we find that contingent control and investor control give a higher payoff to the investor than entrepreneurial control when the signal is sufficiently informative and are therefore feasible when K is too large for entrepreneurial control to be feasible. Moreover, when $\frac{C_B}{S_B} > \frac{C_G}{S_G}$ signal-contingent control gives a higher payoff to the investor than investor control and thus may still be feasible when K is too large for efficient investor control to be feasible (and vice versa if the opposite relation holds). Finally, when both signal-contingent control and efficient investor control are feasible, that is

$$\widehat{\Pi}_I, \Pi_{SC} > K$$

then the parties can effectively choose between the two efficient and feasible regimes. As is clear from our above analysis, the entrepreneur prefers signal-contingent control if $\frac{C_B}{S_B} < \frac{C_G}{S_G}$ and vice versa for the investor.

11.4.3   Comparison with Aghion & Bolton (1992)

Proposition 5(iii) of Aghion & Bolton (1992) is incomplete since it requires the additional condition first outlined by Vauhkonen (2002) which is given by $\frac{C_B}{S_B} > \frac{C_G}{S_G}$ and which we use in our comparison of investor payoffs under the different regimes. When the signals become sufficiently informative and if $\frac{C_B}{S_B} > \frac{C_G}{S_G}$, signal-contingent control dominates unilateral control allocations.

Chapter 12

Unverifiable Information Contracting

12.1 Question 45

Consider a public good problem. There are $N \geq 3$ agents. The indicator variable y is 1 if the good is supplied and 0 if not, and $t_i \in \mathbb{R}$ is the transfer to agent i. The preferences of agent i are quasi-linear: $\theta_i y + t_i$ with $\theta_i \in \mathbb{R}$. We want to study social choice correspondences, $f(\cdot)$, that we can implement in Nash equilibrium.

1. Show that monotonicity implies that $f(\cdot)$ satisfies the following two conditions:

   Condition 1 Consider $\theta = (\theta_1, ..., \theta_N)$ and $(y, t_1, .., t_N) \in f(\theta)$ such that $y = 1$. Consider also $\phi = (\phi_1, ..., \phi_N)$ such that $\phi \geq \theta$ (this means that $\forall i, \phi_i \geq \theta_i$). We then have $(y, t_1, .., t_N) \in f(\phi)$.

   Condition 2 Consider θ and $(y, t_1, .., t_N) \in f(\theta)$ such that $x = 0$. Consider also ϕ such that $\theta \geq \phi$ (this means that $\forall i, \theta_i \geq \phi_i$). We then have $(y, t_1, .., t_N) \in f(\phi)$.

2. Consider now $f(\cdot)$ that satisfies conditions 1 and 2. Show that it is monotonic.

3. Show that $f(\cdot)$ satisfies no veto power. Conclude that $f(\cdot)$ is implementable in Nash equilibrium.

4. Show that we can implement an $f(\cdot)$ that satisfies efficient supply [that is, $\forall \theta$ and $\forall (y, t_1, .., t_N) \in f(\theta)$, $y = 1$ if and only if $\sum_{i=1}^{N} \theta_i \geq 0$] that does not involve transfers when $y = 0$ and that is balanced [i.e., $\forall \theta$ and $\forall (y, t_1, .., t_N) \in f(\theta)$, $\sum_{i=1}^{N} t_i = 0$].

5. Explain why these results are satisfactory if one only cares about efficiency (efficient supply and not throwing money away) but much less satisfactory if one cares about a "fair" sharing of the cost of the public good.

12.2 Question 46

Consider an environment with three individuals (1, 2, and 3) and five outcomes, A, B, C, D, and E. Individual 1 can be of two types, which we call θ_1 and ϕ_1. The same is true for individual 2, who can be of type θ_2 or ϕ_2. Instead, individual 3 has constant preferences. Individual preferences are as follows:

- Individual 1's preferences are summarized by $A \succ B \succ C \succ D \succ E$ when she is of type θ_1, and by $B \succ A \succ E \succ D \succ C$ when he is of type ϕ_1.

- Individual 2's preferences are summarized by $A \succ B \succ C \succ D \succ E$ when she is of type θ_2, and by $B \succ A \succ E \succ D \succ C$ when he is of type ϕ_2.

- Finally, individual 3's preferences are summarized by $E \succ D \succ C \succ B \succ A$.

The social-choice function $f(\cdot)$ is defined as follows:

$$f(\theta_1, \theta_2) = A, \quad f(\theta_1, \phi_2) = D = f(\phi_1, \theta_2), \quad \text{and } f(\phi_1, \phi_2) = B$$

1. Show that f is monotonic and satisfies No Veto Power and is therefore implementable in Nash equilibrium.

2. Show that it cannot be implemented in dominant strategies, however.

12.3 Question 47

Consider an implementation setup without investment but with risk-sharing. Assume the parties, a buyer and a seller, have the following utility functions:

$$u_b[v(q, \theta) - P]$$

$$u_s[P - c(q, \theta)]$$

where u_b, v, and u_s are increasing and concave functions, c is an increasing and convex function, and $v(q, 0) = 0$ and $c(q, 0) = 0$ for all θ's. Contracting takes place before θ is known, trade (P, q) after θ has been observed by both parties.

1. Describe the first best in this setup.

2. Assume that θ is observable but not verifiable, and that the parties cannot commit not to renegotiate but can contractually agree on message-contingent default options and allocations of the entire bargaining power to one party. Construct a revelation game which implements the first best without equilibrium renegotiation.

3. Can a contract without messages but with equilibrium renegotiation implement the first best? Interpret.

12.4 Question 48

Consider the contracting problem seen in sections 12.3.1 and 12.3.2, but, rather than assuming
$$c_H > v_H > c_L > v_L$$
assume
$$v_H > c_H > v_L > c_L$$

1. Compute the first-best outcome.

2. What is the optimal option contract under the assumptions made by Noldeke and Schmidt (1995)?

3. What would happen if option contracts are not feasible because the buyer can always claim that the seller failed to deliver the good, so that we are in the at-will-contracting world of Hart and Moore (1988)?

4. What would happen if, starting from a Hart-Moore world, "trade" rather than "no trade" were to be the result of ex post disagreement?

12.5 Question 49

Consider a buyer-seller model where the seller can make a costly investment i in quality enhancement. Then respective payoff functions are
$$P - cq - i$$
for the seller, and
$$v(q, i) - P$$
for the buyer, where $v_{qi} > 0$; that is, the effect of a rise in quality-enhancement on the buyer valuation $v(\cdot)$ is increasing in the quantity traded q. In addition, P and c stand for price and marginal production cost, as in Chapter 12.

Prices and quantities are assumed to be contractable, while quality is observable but not contractable. The timing of the game is as follows: In stage 0, the parties write an initial contract. In stage 1, the seller chooses i (which then becomes a sunk cost). In stage 2, with probability 0.5, the buyer can make an offer (P, q) while with the remaining probability 0.5 it is the seller who can make an offer (P, q). Finally, in stage 3, the party who did not make the offer in the previous stage can either accept the offer or choose to stick to the initial contract.

1. What are the first-best levels of q and i?

2. What are the equilibrium levels of q and i in the absence of an initial contract [or, equivalently, with an initial contract $(P_0, q_0) = (0, 0)$]?

3. Suppose that the initial contract can only consist in a single pair (P_0, q_0). What will the equilibrium contract be, as well as the associated quality level?

4. Add now to the previous case the following at-will-contracting provision for the buyer. First, when the seller makes the offer in stage 2, the buyer can in stage 3 accept it, accept the initial contract (P_0, q_0), or choose to walk away, that is, choose outcome $(0, 0)$. Second, when the buyer makes the offer in stage 2, the buyer can choose between (P_0, q_0) and $(0, 0)$ if the seller does not accept the buyer's stage-2 offer. What is the impact of this at-will-contracting provision on the equilibrium q and i?

5. If we assume away direct externalities and have payoff functions $v(q) - P$ for the buyer and $P - c(i)q - i$ for the seller [with $c'(i) < 0$], show that choosing a single pair (P_0, q_0) as initial contract is now optimal.

12.5.1   First-Best Solution

The first-best levels of q and i are obtained by maximizing the social surplus

$$\max_{q,i} v(q, i) - cq - i.$$

Taking partial derivatives with respect to q and i we can show that the first-best levels of quantity q^* and investment i^* are given by

$$v_q(q^*, i^*) = c$$
$$v_i(q^*, i^*) = 1$$

where we assume that $v_i, v_q > 0$ and $v_{qq}, v_{ii} < 0$.

12.5.2   No Initial Contract

In stage 2, if the seller can make an offer he solves the following program

$$\max_{P_S, q_S} u_S = P_S - cq_S$$

subject to

$$v(q_S, i) - P_S \geq v(0, i).$$

Noting that the participation constraint of the buyer will be binding, we can substitute an expression for P_S into the objective function and solve the unconstrained problem by differentiating with respect to q_S. As a result we obtain the following expressions for P_S and q_S

$$
\begin{aligned}
P_S &= v(q_S, i) - v(0, i) \\
v_q(q_S, i) &= c.
\end{aligned}
$$

If the buyer can make an offer he solves the program

$$
\max_{P_B, q_B} u_B = v(q_B, i) - P_B
$$

subject to

$$
P_B - c q_B \geq 0.
$$

Analogously, the seller's participation constraint is binding so that we find

$$
\begin{aligned}
P_B &= c q_B \\
v_q(q_B, i) &= c.
\end{aligned}
$$

In stage 1 the seller therefore solves

$$
\max_i E u_s = \frac{1}{2} \left[P_S - c q_S(i) \right] + \frac{1}{2} \left[P_B - c q_B(i) \right] - i.
$$

Substituting the expressions for P_S and P_B the objective function can be written as

$$
\frac{1}{2} \left[v(q_S(i), i) - v(0, i) - c q_S(i) \right] + \frac{1}{2} \left[c q_B(i) - c q_B(i) \right] - i.
$$

Differentiating with respect to i we find that the equilibrium levels of investment i^{no} and quantity q^{no} are characterized by

$$
\begin{aligned}
v_q(q^{no}, i^{no}) &= c \\
v_i(q^{no}, i^{no}) &= 2 + v_i(0, i^{no}).
\end{aligned}
$$

12.5.3 Single-Pair contract

In stage 2, if the seller can make an offer he solves the following program

$$
\max_{P_S, q_S} u_S = P_S - c q_S
$$

subject to

$$
v(q_S, i) - P_S \geq v(q_0, i) - P_0.
$$

Noting that the participation constraint of the buyer will be binding, we can substitute an expression for P_S into the objective function and solve the unconstrained problem by differentiating with respect to q_S. As a result we obtain the following expressions for P_S and q_S

$$
\begin{aligned}
P_S &= P_0 + v(q_S, i) - v(q_0, i) \\
v_q(q_S, i) &= c.
\end{aligned}
$$

If the buyer can make an offer he solves the program

$$\max_{P_B, q_B} u_B = v(q_B, i) - P_B$$

subject to

$$P_B - cq_B \geq P_0 - cq_0.$$

Analogously, the seller's participation constraint is binding so that we find

$$
\begin{aligned}
P_B &= P_0 + cq_B - cq_0 \\
v_q(q_B, i) &= c.
\end{aligned}
$$

In stage 1 the seller therefore solves

$$\max_i Eu_s = \frac{1}{2}[P_S - cq_S(i)] + \frac{1}{2}[P_B - cq_B(i)] - i.$$

Substituting the expressions for P_S and P_B the objective function can be written as

$$\frac{1}{2}[P_0 + v(q_S(i), i) - v(q_0, i) - cq_S(i)] + \frac{1}{2}[P_0 + cq_B(i) - cq_0 - cq_B(i)] - i.$$

Differentiating with respect to i we find that the equilibrium levels of investment i^{si} and quantity q^{si} are characterized by

$$
\begin{aligned}
v_q(q^{si}, i^{si}) &= c \\
v_i(q^{si}, i^{si}) &= 2 + v_i(q_0, i^{si}).
\end{aligned}
$$

Before stage 1, the parties set the initial contract (P_0, q_0) to have q^{si} and i^{si} to be as close as possible to the first-best levels q^* and i^*. Hence, q_0 should be set such that

$$v_i(q_0, i^{si}) = -1.$$

However, since we usually assume that v is increasing in i, the best the parties can do is to set q_0 such that $v_i(q_0, i^{si})$ is as low as possible since $v_{qi} > 0$. Choosing the lowest possible amount for q_0 we have

$$q_0 = 0.$$

The initial price P_0 solely serves to divide the surplus between buyer and seller and could, for example, be set to satisfy the ex ante participation constraint of the buyer so that $P_0 = v(q_0, i^{si})$. Since $q_0 = 0$ the equilibrium values for q and i are the same as if there was no initial contract.

12.5.4 At-Will-Contracting Provision

If the seller is allowed to make an offer in stage 2, he solves the following problem

$$\max_{P_S, q_S} u_S = P_S - cq_S$$

subject to

$$v(q_S, i) - P_S \geq v(q_0, i) - P_0$$
$$v(q_S, i) - P_S \geq v(0, i).$$

Clearly, one of the constraints is binding while the other is slack. In particular we have

$$
\begin{aligned}
P_S &= v(q_S, i) + \min\{P_0 - v(q_0, i), -v(0, i)\} \\
&= v(q_S, i) - \max\{v(q_0, i) - P_0, v(0, i)\}.
\end{aligned}
$$

The optimal quantity level can be obtained by differentiating the unconstrained problem with respect to q_S

$$v_q(q_S, i) = c.$$

If the buyer is allowed to make an offer and the seller rejects, the buyer has the choice between (P_0, q_0) and $(0, 0)$. He chooses the former if and only if

$$v(q_0, i) - P_0 \geq v(0, i)$$

and the latter if

$$v(q_0, i) - P_0 < v(0, i).$$

Thus, in stage 2, if $v(q_0, i) - P_0 \geq v(0, i)$ the buyer solves the following program

$$\max_{P_B, q_B} u_B = v(q_B, i) - P_{B1}$$

subject to

$$P_{B1} - cq_{B1} \geq P_0 - cq_0.$$

The conditions that characterizes the optimal price and quantity choices are

$$
\begin{aligned}
P_{B1} &= P_0 + cq_{B1} - cq_0 \\
v_q(q_{B1}, i) &= c.
\end{aligned}
$$

On the other hand, if $v(q_0, i) - P_0 < v(0, i)$ we obtain

$$
\begin{aligned}
P_{B2} &= cq_{B2} \\
v_q(q_{B2}, i) &= c.
\end{aligned}
$$

As a result, in stage 1 the seller solves

$$\max_i Eu_S = \frac{1}{2}\left[P_S - cq_S(i)\right] + \frac{1}{2}\left[(P_{B1} - cq_{B1}(i))\mathbf{I} + (P_{B2} - cq_{B2}(i))(1 - \mathbf{I})\right] - i$$

with the indicator function $\mathbf{I} = \mathbf{I}(v(q_0, i) - P_0 \geq v(0, i))$. Now, substituting for P_S, P_{B1} and P_{B2} we obtain

$$\max_i Eu_S = \frac{1}{2}\left[v(q_S, i) - \max\{v(q_0, i) - P_0, v(0, i)\} - cq_S(i)\right] + \frac{1}{2}(P_0 - cq_0)\mathbf{I} - i.$$

Looking at the expression above it is clear that additional incentives for investment arise from the contracting-at-will provision which introduces a discontinuity in the objective function of the seller. The investment incentives for the seller are optimal if (P_0, q_0) is set in such a way that $P_0 - cq_0$ is as large as possible subject to the constraint $P_0 = v(q_0, i^*) - v(0, i^*)$ where i^* is the first-best efficient level of investment determined before. Substituting the constraint we maximize the following expression with respect to q_0

$$v(q_0, i^*) - v(0, i^*) - cq_0.$$

Differentiating we obtain the expression that characterizes q_0

$$v_q(q_0, i^*) = c$$

so that we have $q_0 = q^* = q_S$. Thus, at the first-best efficient level i^* the seller's payoff is given by

$$Eu_S = v(q_0, i^*) - v(0, i^*) - cq_0 - i^*$$

where we substituted the expressions found above. It is easy to show that the seller will never choose a level of investment $i > i^*$. Furthermore, if, for example, $v(0, i) = 0$ then the seller will never choose $i < i^*$ and choose the first-best efficient level i^*.

The introduction of a two-pair contract and an at-will-contracting provision ensures that the first-best levels of q and i are chosen by the parties.

12.5.5   No Direct Externalities

In stage 2, if the seller can make an offer he solves the following program

$$\max_{P_S, q_S} u_S = P_S - c(i)q_S$$

subject to

$$v(q_S) - P_S \geq v(q_0) - P_0.$$

The participation constraint of the buyer will be binding so we can substitute an expression for P_S into the objective function and solve the unconstrained problem by differentiating with respect to q_S. As a result we obtain the following expressions for P_S and q_S

$$\begin{aligned} P_S &= P_0 + v(q_S) - v(q_0) \\ v'(q_S) &= c(i). \end{aligned}$$

If the buyer can make an offer he solves the program

$$\max_{P_B, q_B} u_B = v(q_B) - P_B$$

subject to

$$P_B - c(i)q_B \geq P_0 - c(i)q_0.$$

Analogously, the seller's participation constraint is binding so that we find

$$P_B = P_0 + c(i)q_B - c(i)q_0$$
$$v'(q_B) = c.$$

In stage 1 the seller therefore solves

$$\max_i Eu_s = \frac{1}{2}[P_S - cq_S)] + \frac{1}{2}[P_B - cq_B] - i.$$

Substituting the expressions for P_S and P_B the objective function can be written as

$$\frac{1}{2}[P_0 + v(q_S) - v(q_0) - c(i)q_S] + \frac{1}{2}[P_0 + c(i)q_B - c(i)q_0 - c(i)q_B] - i.$$

Differentiating with respect to i we find that the equilibrium levels of investment i^{ne} and quantity q^{ne} are characterized by

$$v'(q^{ne}) = c(i)$$
$$-c'(i)q^{ne} = 2 + c'(i)q_0.$$

With the new preferences the first-best levels of quantity and investment are characterized by

$$v'(q^*) = c(i^*)$$
$$-c'(i^*)q^* = 1.$$

Thus, the parties optimally set q_0 such that

$$q_0 = -\frac{1}{c'(i)}$$

which is feasible since $c'(i) < 0$. Finally, we set $P_0 = v(q_0)$ to satisfy the ex ante participation constraint of the buyer.

12.6 Question 50

Consider a simplified version of the problem in Segal (1999) and Hart & Moore (1999), with only two widgets, widget 1 and widget 2. Widget 1 costs the seller 0 to produce, while widget 2 costs the seller 1 to produce. Valuations are uncertain, however: in the "good state of nature," widget 1 gives the buyer utility $v > 1$ while widget 2 gives her zero utility; the "bad state of nature" is the opposite case, in that it is widget 2 that gives the buyer utility $v > 1$ while widget 1 gives her zero utility (note that surplus is thus higher in the good state). At investment cost i^2, the seller can induce a probability i that the state of nature is good (and thus $1 - i$ that it is bad).

1. Derive the first-best in this environment.

2. Assume the buyer has full bargaining power in renegotiation. What will be the investment level without the contract if payoffs are mutually observable ex post?

3. Explain how a contract can induce the first best if widgets can be contractually identified by their number ex post and if the parties can commit not to renegotiate the contract.

4. Assume widgets can be contractually identified by their number both ex post and ex ante, but the parties cannot commit not to renegotiate the contract (and the buyer has full bargaining power in the renegotiation). To what extent does contracting reduce the underinvestment of the seller relative to the first best? (Following the lines of the proof detailed in section 12.3.4.2, look at the two following incentive constraints: the one where the buyer considers claiming that the state is bad while it is in fact good, and the one where the seller considers claiming the state is good while it is in fact bad).

5. Discuss this result and compare it with Segal's result.

12.6.1   First-Best Outcome

The first-best allocation solves

$$
\begin{aligned}
\max_i S(i) &= \max_i \left\{ \Pr\left(\theta = G\right)(v - c_1) + \Pr\left(\theta = B\right)(v - c_2) - i^2 \right\} \\
&= \max_i \left\{ v - 1 + i - i^2 \right\}
\end{aligned}
$$

where $\theta = G, B$ denotes the state of nature. Thus, we obtain

$$
i^* = \frac{1}{2}.
$$

12.6.2   Null Contract with Renegotiation

Since the buyer has full bargaining power in renegotiation he sets prices subject to the seller just to be willing to trade the right widget, that is widget 1 in the good state and widget 2 in the bad state with prices $P_{1G} = c_1$ and $P_{2B} = c_2$. The seller therefore maximizes

$$
\begin{aligned}
\pi(i) &= i\left(P_{1G} - c_1\right) + (1 - i)\left(P_{2B} - c_2\right) - i^2 \\
&= -i^2
\end{aligned}
$$

and so we obtain

$$
i^{R0} = 0.
$$

12.6.3 No Renegotiation

If the parties can commit not to renegotiate an ex ante contract then the first best can be achieved. For example, they could specify a mechanism that gives the seller the right to make a take-it-or-leave-it offer to the buyer after the state has been realized. In this case the seller would offer a price $P_{1G} = v$ for widget 1 in the good state and $P_{2B} = v$ for widget 2 in the bad state and the buyer would accept the offer. As a result the seller's investment decision is

$$\max_i \pi(i) = \max_i \left\{ i \left(P_{1G} - c_1 \right) + (1 - i) \left(P_{2B} - c_2 \right) - i^2 \right\}$$
$$= \max_i \left\{ iv + (1 - i)(v - 1) - i^2 \right\}$$

which results in the first-best investment choice

$$i^{NR} = \frac{1}{2}.$$

Note that this mechanism could not be implemented if renegotiation were possible. The buyer could always reject the seller's offer and then rely on renegotiation to ensure herself a higher payoff, leaving no incentives to invest to the seller.

12.6.4 Contracting with Renegotiation

Define a state of nature (θ, τ) where τ is the permutation where the widgets are in the right order. Let τ' be the permutation that switches the order of the two widgets. That is to say under permutation τ widget 1 is labeled as widget 1 and widget 2 is labeled as widget 2, whereas under permutation τ' widget 1 is labeled as widget 2 and widget 2 is labeled as widget 1. Take any mechanism M that upon a pair of non-matching announcements about the state of nature by the parties about the state prescribes a starting point of renegotiation where the buyer has to pay the seller an amount $\tilde{P}$ and where widget labeled as widget n is traded with probability x_n while no trade happens with probability

$$1 - \sum_{n=1}^{2} x_n \geq 0.$$

Consider the following incentive constraints.

1. In state of nature (B, τ') the seller should not play as if the state of nature were (G, τ).

2. In state of nature (G, τ) the buyer should not play as if the state of nature were (B, τ').

The incentive constraint in state of nature (B, τ) for the seller is

$$P(B, \tau') - c_2 \geq \tilde{P} - x_1 c_1 - x_2 c_2.$$

Now, for the second incentive constraint in state of nature (G, τ') the seller's default option cannot be less than what he gets in equilibrium, since if the seller were worse off the buyer would be better off. Thus, the following inequality must hold:

$$\widetilde{P} - x_1 c_2 - x_2 c_1 \geq P(G, \tau) - c_1.$$

The two inequalities imply

$$P(B, \tau') - P(G, \tau) \geq c_2 - c_1 - x_1 c_1 - x_2 c_2 + x_1 c_2 + x_2 c_1.$$

Rearranging and substituting values for c_1 and c_2 we obtain

$$P(B, \tau') - P(G, \tau) \geq 1 + x_1 - x_2$$

which has to hold for every (τ, τ') pair. The seller's ex ante investment problem is therefore to maximize

$$\pi(i) = i \left[\frac{1}{2} P(G, \tau) + \frac{1}{2} P(G, \tau') - c_1 \right]$$
$$+ (1-i) \left[\frac{1}{2} P(B, \tau) + \frac{1}{2} P(B, \tau') - c_2 \right] - i^2.$$

$\Leftrightarrow$

$$\pi(i) = \frac{1}{2} \left[P(B, \tau) + P(B, \tau') - 2 \right]$$
$$- \frac{i}{2} \left[P(B, \tau') - P(G, \tau) + P(B, \tau) - P(G, \tau') - 2 \right] - i^2.$$

Since the combined incentive constraints have to hold for every (τ, τ') pair we can substitute the expression we found from combining the incentive constraints. The resulting objective function is

$$\frac{1}{2} \left[P(B, \tau) + P(B, \tau') - 2 \right] - i \left[x_1 - x_2 \right] - i^2.$$

The first order condition therefore yields

$$i^R \leq \frac{x_2 - x_1}{2}.$$

Clearly, for this solution to be as close as possible to the first best, we must have

$$x_2 = 1 + x_1$$

which combined with the fact that x_1 and x_2 cannot be greater than 1 implies

$$\begin{aligned} x_2^R &= 1 \\ x_1^R &= 0. \end{aligned}$$

In other words, as the realization of the seller's cost fall from 1 to 0, the seller's payoff rises by at most $x_1 - x_2$ and so investment incentives are maximized when this difference is as large as possible, i.e., equal to 1.

12.6.5 Discussion

In Segal's and Hart & Moore's model each inefficient future trade creates a hold-up opportunity and therefore introduces a new set of incentive constraints. The greater the number of inefficient trades, the more incentive constraints need to be satisfied to prevent the parties from misrepresenting the efficient trade, and the lower the value of contracting. The value of contracting approaches zero when the number of inefficient trades becomes infinitely large, and so the parties might as well stick to the null contract.

In the present model, after contracting there are only two inefficient trades that can create hold-up and require additional incentive constraints, namely (B, τ') and (G, τ) and thus contracting still offers some improvement over the null contract.

12.7 Question 51

Consider the Aghion-Tirole (1997) model described in Chapter 12. Assume quadratic effort costs:

1. Compute the principal's payoff with and without delegation. Derive the comparative statics of the maximum of these two payoffs with respect to α and β. Discuss.

2. What is the effect of relaxing the assumption that $\alpha > 0$?

3. What is the effect of relaxing the assumption that, if uninformed, the agent would not "choose a project at random"? Specifically, call $\gamma_P < 0$ the principal's payoff from the agent's random choice, while $\gamma_A > 0$ the associated agent's payoff. What is the outcome of the game under these assumptions?

12.7.1 Aghion-Tirole with Quadratic Effort Costs

We use H, h instead of B, b which is used inconsistently in section 12.4.2. To ensure uniqueness and stability in equilibrium following Aghion & Tirole (1997) we assume that

$$\alpha h H < c_A c_P$$
$$\beta h H < c_A c_P.$$

To rule out uninteresting corner solutions we make the following stricter assumptions

$$h < c_A$$
$$H < c_P.$$

No Delegation

The payoffs of the two players without delegation are

$$U_P^{NO} = EH + (1 - E)e\alpha H - \frac{c_P}{2}E^2$$
$$U_A^{NO} = E\beta h + (1 - E)eh - \frac{c_A}{2}e^2.$$

The best-response functions are given by

$$E = \frac{H(1 - e\alpha)}{c_P}$$
$$e = \frac{h(1 - E)}{c_A}.$$

Solving this system we obtain

$$E^{NO} = \frac{H(c_A - h\alpha)}{c_A c_P - Hh\alpha}$$
$$e^{NO} = \frac{h(c_P - H)}{c_A c_P - Hh\alpha}.$$

Using these expressions we can compute the principal's payoff without delegation

$$U_P^{NO} = \frac{H^2(c_A - h\alpha)}{c_A c_P - Hh\alpha} + \frac{Hh\alpha(c_P - H)^2}{(c_A c_P - Hh\alpha)^2} - \frac{c_P H^2(c_A - h\alpha)^2}{2(c_A c_P - Hh\alpha)^2}.$$

The comparative statics with respect to α and β are

$$\frac{\partial U_P^{NO}}{\partial \alpha} = \frac{c_P c_A^2 Hh(c_P - H)^2}{(c_A c_P - Hh\alpha)^3} > 0$$
$$\frac{\partial U_P^{NO}}{\partial \beta} = 0.$$

Delegation

The payoffs of the two players under delegation are

$$U_P^{DEL} = e\alpha H + (1 - e)EH - \frac{c_P}{2}E^2$$
$$U_A^{DEL} = eh + (1 - e)E\beta h - \frac{c_A}{2}e^2.$$

The best-response functions are given by

$$E = \frac{H(1 - e)}{c_P}$$
$$e = \frac{h(1 - E\beta)}{c_A}.$$

Solving this system we obtain

$$E^{DEL} = \frac{H(c_A - h)}{c_A c_P - Hh\beta}$$

$$e^{DEL} = \frac{h(c_P - \beta H)}{c_A c_P - Hh\beta}.$$

Using these expression we can compute the principal's payoff under delegation

$$U_P^{DEL} = \frac{Hh\alpha(c_P - H\beta)}{c_A c_P - Hh\beta} + \frac{c_P H^2(c_A - h)^2}{2(c_A c_P - Hh\beta)^2}.$$

The comparative statics with respect to α and β are

$$\frac{\partial U_P^{DEL}}{\partial \alpha} = \frac{Hh(c_P - \beta H)}{c_A c_P - Hh\beta} > 0$$

$$\frac{\partial U_P^{DEL}}{\partial \beta} = \frac{c_P H^2 h(c_A - h)\left[H(c_A - h) - \alpha(c_A c_P - Hh\beta)\right]}{(c_A c_P - Hh\beta)^3}.$$

As a result, the principal's maximum payoff is always increasing in α. The sign of the last derivative above is given by

$$sign\left(\frac{\partial U_P^{DEL}}{\partial \beta}\right) = sign\left(H(c_A - h) - \alpha(c_A c_P - Hh\beta)\right).$$

Discussion

Under both delegation and no delegation the principal benefits from an increase in the congruence parameter α. Under delegation the increase in α does not influence effort choices but the principal obtains a higher payoff when the agent implements his preferred project. Under no delegation an increase in α also raises E^{NO} and lowers e^{NO} but the effect is still positive.

When there is no delegation the congruence parameter β has no influence on efforts and also does not affect the principal's payoff. Thus its effect is zero. On the other hand under delegation it influences the effort choices of the two parties. An increase in β reduces E^{DEL} and increases e^{DEL} so that the effect on the principal's payoff is ambiguous.

12.7.2 Strong Conflict of Interest

No Delegation

If $\alpha \leq 0$, then without delegation the principal will not follow the advice of the agent since this would yield a weakly negative payoff. Instead he will choose not to undertake any project. Hence, without delegation the payoffs now are given by

$$U_P^{NO} = EH - \frac{c_P}{2}E^2$$

$$U_A^{NO} = EH\beta - \frac{c_A}{2}e^2.$$

As a result the equilibrium effort choices are

$$E^{NO} = \frac{H}{c_P}$$
$$e^{NO} = 0.$$

The principal's equilibrium payoff is given by

$$U_P^{NO} = \frac{H^2}{2c_P}$$

which does not vary with respect to α or β.

Delegation

With delegation the situation is exactly the same as before. Since the principal cedes formal authority to the agent he cannot prevent the agent from choosing his favorite project. As a result, all the conclusions of the previous sections still hold.

12.7.3   Random Choice of Project

When both parties are uninformed the agent now chooses a project at random. If the principal is uninformed he will prefer to undertake no project at all or let the agent choose a project if the latter is informed.

No Delegation

If we assume that the principal can observe whether or not the agent is informed, nothing is changed relative to the benchmark case. However, when the principal cannot observe if the agent is informed he will choose to follow the agent's advice if and only if

$$e\alpha H + (1 - e)\gamma_P \geq 0,$$

or more explicitly, the agent's equilibrium effort has to be sufficiently high

$$e \geq -\frac{\gamma_P}{\alpha H - \gamma_P}.$$

Otherwise the principal will ignore the agent's recommendation and choose no project at all when uninformed and we are back to the same situation as in the previous section.

If the principal follows the advice of the agent the payoffs for the players are given by

$$U_P^{NO} = EH + (1 - E)e\alpha H + (1 - E)(1 - e)\gamma_P - \frac{c_P}{2}E^2$$
$$U_A^{NO} = E\beta h + (1 - E)eh + (1 - E)(1 - e)\gamma_A - \frac{c_A}{2}e^2.$$

The best-response functions are

$$E = \frac{H(1 - e\alpha) - \gamma_P(1 - e)}{c_P}$$

$$e = \frac{(h - \gamma_A)(1 - E)}{c_A}$$

and the resulting equilibrium effort choices are given by

$$E^{NO} = \frac{c_A(H - \gamma_P) - (h - \gamma_A)(\alpha H - \gamma_P)}{c_A c_P - (h - \gamma_A)(\alpha H - \gamma_P)}$$

$$e^{NO} = \frac{(h - \gamma_A)(c_P - H + \gamma_P)}{c_A c_P - (h - \gamma_A)(\alpha H - \gamma_P)}.$$

As mentioned before, for this to be a solution we need

$$e^{NO} \geq -\frac{\gamma_P}{\alpha H - \gamma_P}$$

or equivalently

$$\alpha \geq -\frac{\gamma_P\left[c_A c_P - (h - \gamma_A)(c_P - H + \gamma_P)\right]}{H(h - \gamma_A)(c_P - H)}.$$

Delegation

Under delegation the agent may choose a project at random when he is uninformed. We distinguish between two cases.

Case 1: $\gamma_A > \beta H$ In this case the agent prefers to choose a project at random rather than follow the principal's advice when the latter is informed. The payoffs are therefore given by

$$U_P^{DEL} = e\alpha H + (1 - e)\gamma_P - \frac{c_P}{2}E^2$$

$$U_A^{DEL} = eh + (1 - e)\gamma_A - \frac{c_A}{2}e^2.$$

The outcome of the game under these assumptions is

$$E^{DEL} = 0$$

$$e^{DEL} = \frac{h - \gamma_A}{c_A}$$

$$U_P^{DEL} = \frac{c_A \gamma_P + (h - \gamma_A)(\alpha H - \gamma_P)}{c_A}$$

and the principal's equilibrium payoff is increasing in α.

Case 2: $\gamma_A \leq \beta H$ The agent now only chooses a project at random if and only if neither of the players is informed. The payoffs are

$$
U_P^{DEL} = e\alpha H + (1-e)EH + (1-e)(1-E)\gamma_P - \frac{c_P}{2}E^2
$$

$$
U_A^{DEL} = eh + (1-e)E\beta h + (1-e)(1-E)\gamma_A - \frac{c_A}{2}e^2.
$$

From the first order conditions we obtain

$$
E = \frac{(H-\gamma_P)(1-e)}{c_P}
$$

$$
e = \frac{h(1-\beta E) - \gamma_A(1-E)}{c_A}
$$

and consequently

$$
E^{DEL} = \frac{(H-\gamma_P)(c_A - h + \gamma_A)}{c_A c_P - (H-\gamma_P)(h\beta - \gamma_A)}
$$

$$
e^{DEL} = \frac{c_P(h-\gamma_A) - (H-\gamma_P)(h\beta - \gamma_A)}{c_A c_P - (H-\gamma_P)(h\beta - \gamma_A)}.
$$

Chapter 13

Markets and Contracts

13.1 Question 52

Consider an agent with CARA utility function

$$-e^{-\eta(w-ca^2/2)}$$

where w is monetary compensation and a is effort. Her certainty-equivalent reservation wage is w_0. Output $q = a + \varepsilon$, where ε has a normal distribution $N(0, \sigma^2)$. Two risk-neutral principals (who do not observe a) are interested in q: principal 1 gets a benefit $B_1 q$ and principal 2 gets a benefit $B_2 q$. The agent could be a government agency, and the principals could be political interest groups.

1. Assuming that the principals can join forces and offer the agent a contract $w = t + sq$ to maximize $(B_1 + B_2)q$, what is the optimal contract for them: (a) when they can observe and contract on a and (b) when they cannot observe a?

2. Assume that each principal i independently offers a contract $w_i = t_i + s_i q$, that contract offers are simultaneous, and that the agent can only either accept both contracts [in which case she obtains $t_1 + t_2 + (s_1 + s_2)q$] or refuse both. Compute the equilibrium level of $s_1 + s_2$, and compare it with the level of s obtained in part 1. Discuss.

13.1.1 Observable and Contractible Action

When the principals can join forces and contract on a, they solve the following problem

$$\max_{a,w}(B_1 + B_2)a - w$$

subject to

$$CE = E(w) - \frac{\eta}{2}\text{var}(w) - \frac{c}{2}a^2 \geq w_0.$$

Thus the first-best effort level is given by

$$a^* = \frac{B_1 + B_2}{c}$$

and the optimal contract enforces this effort level by paying a fixed wage w when $a = a^*$. The fixed wage just satisfies the participation constraint

$$w = w_0 + \frac{(B_1 + B_2)^2}{2c}.$$

As usual, when actions are contractible the optimal contract fully insures the agent against risk and implements the efficient effort level.

13.1.2　Unobservable or Non-Contractible Action

When a is unobservable (or non-contractible) the principals jointly solve

$$\max_{a,t,s}(B_1 + B_2 - s)a - t$$

subject to

$$CE = t + sa - \frac{\eta}{2}s^2\sigma^2 - \frac{c}{2}a^2 \geq w_0$$

and

$$a \in \arg\max CE.$$

The incentive compatibility constraint implies $a = \frac{s}{c}$. As usual, we rewrite the problem to solve the following unconstrained maximization problem

$$\max_{s}(B_1 + B_2)\frac{s}{c} - \frac{\eta}{2}s^2\sigma^2 - \frac{s^2}{2c}.$$

Thus the optimal (second-best) joint contract is

$$s^J = \frac{B_1 + B_2}{1 + \eta\sigma^2 c}$$

$$t^J = w_0 + \frac{(B_1 + B_2)^2(\eta\sigma^2 c - 1)}{2c(1 + \eta\sigma^2 c)^2}.$$

Finally, the equilibrium effort

$$a^J = \frac{B_1 + B_2}{(1 + \eta\sigma^2 c)c}.$$

is lower than first-best effort a^*.

13.1.3 Common Agency

Since the problem is symmetric for the two principals we can focus on principal 1 who is now faced with the following maximization problem

$$\max_{a,t_1,s_1} (B_1 - s_1)a - t_1$$

subject to

$$CE = t_1 + t_2 + (s_1 + s_2)a - \frac{\eta}{2}(s_1 + s_2)^2\sigma^2 - \frac{c}{2}a^2 \geq w_0$$

and

$$a \in \arg\max CE.$$

Note that in the Nash equilibrium each principal takes the choice of the other principal (t_j, s_j) as given. The incentive compatibility constraint implies

$$a = \frac{s_1 + s_2}{c}.$$

Using the participation constraint and taking (t_2, s_2) as given we solve the unconstrained problem

$$\max_{s_1} \left\{ (B_1 - s_1)\frac{s_1 + s_2}{c} - \frac{(\eta\sigma^2 c - 1)}{2c}(s_1 + s_2)^2 \right\}.$$

The best-response function is

$$s_1 = \frac{B_1 - \eta\sigma^2 cs_2}{1 + \eta\sigma^2 c}$$

and similarly for principal 2

$$s_2 = \frac{B_2 - \eta\sigma^2 cs_1}{1 + \eta\sigma^2 c}.$$

Solving this system of equations we obtain the Nash equilibrium values

$$s_1^N = \frac{(1 + \eta\sigma^2 c)B_1 - \eta\sigma^2 cB_2}{1 + 2\eta\sigma^2 c}$$

$$s_2^N = \frac{(1 + \eta\sigma^2 c)B_2 - \eta\sigma^2 cB_1}{1 + 2\eta\sigma^2 c}.$$

We can compare the sum of the Nash equilibrium level to the level obtained in the situation where the principals jointly offer a contract to the agent. Here we have

$$s_1^N + s_2^N = \frac{B_1 + B_2}{1 + 2\eta\sigma^2 c} < \frac{B_1 + B_2}{1 + \eta\sigma^2 c} = s^J.$$

As a result, the equilibrium effort a^N under common agency is also lower than under a joint contract a^J

$$a^N = \frac{B_1 + B_2}{(1 + 2\eta\sigma^2 c)\,c} < \frac{B_1 + B_2}{(1 + \eta\sigma^2 c)\,c} = a^J.$$

Common agency introduces inefficiency over and above that resulting from the non-verifiability of actions. This occurs because when choosing the incentive contract each principal attempts to free-ride on the incentives provided to the agent by the other principal.

13.2   Question 53

Consider an agent who works for two risk-neutral principals ($i = 1, 2$) and produces $q_i = a_i + \varepsilon_i$ for principal i where a_i is effort and the ε_i's are independently and normally distributed with mean 0 and variance σ_i^2. The agent's utility function is

$$-e^{-\eta(w - a_1^2/2 - a_2^2/2)}$$

where w is monetary compensation. Principals are restricted to making simultaneous noncooperative contract offers that are linear in output levels. The agent can accept 0, 1, or both contracts. Her certainty-equivalent reservation wage is 0.

1. Assume each principal can only observe his own output q_i and thus offers a contract $w_i = t_i + s_i q_i$. Compute the Nash equilibrium contracts and effort levels. How do they compare to the optimal contract where the principals can join forces and offer contracts that maximize their joint payoff? Discuss.

2. Assume each principal can observe both output levels and thus offers a contract $w_i = t_i + s_i q_i + f_i q_j$. Compute the equilibrium contracts and effort levels. Compare with the solution in 1. above.

13.3   Question 54

Consider a public project that a firm can build at cost $\theta \in [\underline{\theta}, \overline{\theta}]$. The firm knows the realization of θ, but regional governments believe it to be distributed according to a density $f(\theta)$ and cumulative distribution function $F(\theta)$ [with $F(\theta)/f(\theta)$ nondecreasing in θ].

There are two regional governments ($i = 1, 2$), with social benefit S_i in region i (positive or negative, depending on employment or environmental considerations, for example). Each government i can set a (negative or positive) transfer T_i the firm receives if and only if it builds the project.

The firm's payoff is

$$u = d(T_1 + T_2 - \theta)$$

where $d = 1$ if the project is built and 0 otherwise. Government i's payoff is

$$V_i = d[S_i - (1 + \lambda)T_i] + u/2$$

where λ is the shadow cost of public funds.

1. What is the first-best value θ^* such that the project should be built if and only if $\theta \leq \theta^*$?

2. Assuming from now on that θ is private information to the firm, consider first the case where the regional governments join forces and choose $T = T_1 + T_2$ so as to maximize $V_1 + V_2$. Derive the optimal transfer T and the value θ^c such that the firm builds the project if and only if $\theta \leq \theta^c$.

3. Now assume that the regional governments set the T_i's noncooperatively. Derive the equilibrium T_i's and the value θ^{nc} such that the firm builds the project if and only if $\theta \leq \theta^{nc}$.

4. Discuss and compare the answers obtained in parts 1, 2, and 3 above.

13.3.1 First-Best Solution

The first-best solution maximizes the joint surplus $V_1 + V_2$

$$\max_{d, T_1, T_2} d\left[S_1 + S_2 - \lambda\left(T_1 + T_2\right) - \theta\right].$$

Hence, since $d \in \{0, 1\}$ the project will be built if and only if

$$\theta \leq S_1 + S_2 - \lambda(T_1 + T_2).$$

The firm will only be willing to build the project if

$$T_1 + T_2 - \theta \geq 0.$$

The optimal contract leaves the firm with no surplus and hence we know that the first-best value of θ^* is given by

$$\theta^* = \frac{S_1 + S_2}{1 + \lambda}$$

below which the project will be built. Note that θ^* takes the shadow cost of public funds into account.

13.3.2 Joint Contract

When the principals can join forces they solve the following problem

$$\max_T \int_{\underline{\theta}}^{\overline{\theta}} d(S_1 + S_2 - \lambda T - \theta)f(\theta)d\theta$$

subject to

$$d(T - \theta) \geq 0$$

and

$$d = \arg \max_{\widetilde{d}} \widetilde{d}(T - \theta)$$

for all θ. From the incentive compatibility constraint we know that for a given T the firm will undertake the project if and only if $\theta \leq T$. Hence the governments maximize their joint surplus with respect to T

$$\int_{\underline{\theta}}^{T} (S_1 + S_2 - \lambda T - \theta) f(\theta) d\theta.$$

Using integration by parts this expression can be rewritten as

$$[S_1 + S_2 - (1 + \lambda) T] F(T) + \int_{\underline{\theta}}^{T} F(\theta) d\theta.$$

The first order condition yields

$$[S_1 + S_2 - (1 + \lambda) T] f(T) - (1 + \lambda) F(T) + F(T) = 0.$$

The optimal contract leaves no surplus to the firm, so $T = \theta^c$ which from the first order condition is given by

$$T = \theta^c = \frac{S_1 + S_2}{1 + \lambda} - \frac{\lambda}{1 + \lambda} \frac{F(\theta^c)}{f(\theta^c)}.$$

13.3.3   Common Agency

The governments non-cooperatively choose T_1 and T_2. Taking T_2 as given government 1 solves

$$\max_{T_1} \int_{\underline{\theta}}^{\overline{\theta}} d \left\{ S_1 - \frac{1}{2} \left[(1 + 2\lambda) T_1 - T_2 + \theta \right] \right\} f(\theta) d\theta$$

subject to

$$d(T_1 + T_2 - \theta) \geq 0$$

and

$$d = \arg \max d(T_1 + T_2 - \theta)$$

for all θ. From the incentive compatibility constraint we know that for a given T the firm will undertake the project if and only if $\theta \leq T_1 + T_2$. Hence government 1 maximizes the following expression

$$\int_{\underline{\theta}}^{T_1 + T_2} \left\{ S_1 - \frac{1}{2} \left[(1 + 2\lambda) T_1 - T_2 + \theta \right] \right\} f(\theta) d\theta.$$

Using integration by parts this expression can be rewritten as

$$\left[\left\{S_1 - \frac{1}{2}\left[(1+2\lambda)T_1 - T_2 + \theta\right]\right\}F(\theta)\right]_{\underline{\theta}}^{T_1+T_2} + \frac{1}{2}\int_{\underline{\theta}}^{T_1+T_2}F(\theta)d\theta.$$

We can simplify this expression to obtain

$$[S_1 - (1+\lambda)T_1]F(T_1+T_2) + \frac{1}{2}\int_{\underline{\theta}}^{T_1+T_2}F(\theta)d\theta.$$

Taking the derivative with respect to T_1 we obtain the first order condition for government 1

$$[S_1 - (1+\lambda)T_1]f(T_1+T_2) - (1+\lambda)F(T_1+T_2) + \frac{1}{2}F(T_1+T_2) = 0.$$

Rearranging we obtain the best-response payment T_1 for government 1

$$T_1 = \frac{S_1}{1+\lambda} - \frac{1+2\lambda}{2(1+\lambda)}\frac{F(T_1+T_2)}{f(T_1+T_2)}$$

and by symmetry for government 2

$$T_2 = \frac{S_2}{1+\lambda} - \frac{1+2\lambda}{2(1+\lambda)}\frac{F(T_1+T_2)}{f(T_1+T_2)}.$$

The optimal set of contracts leaves no surplus to the firm, so $T_1 + T_2 = \theta^{nc}$ which from the first order condition is given by

$$\theta^{nc} = \frac{S_1+S_2}{1+\lambda} - \frac{1+2\lambda}{1+\lambda}\frac{F(\theta^{nc})}{f(\theta^{nc})}.$$

13.3.4 Comparison and Discussion

Noting that the shadow cost of public funds is positive $\lambda > 0$ and that $\frac{F(\theta)}{f(\theta)}$ is non-decreasing in θ we can establish the following relationship

$$\theta^* > \theta^c > \theta^{nc}.$$

As a result the project will be undertaken fewer times than would be efficient when the cost parameter θ is private information and when governments do not coordinate their actions. There are two inefficiencies at work here. First, the non-observability of the cost parameter θ forces governments to offer a type-independent transfer T^c which is inefficiently low. Second, when governments behave non-cooperatively each government i attempts to free-ride on the payment provided by the other government T_j^{nc} resulting in an even lower sum of payments and thus a lower cut-off value for the cost parameter.

Bibliography

Aghion, P., and P. Bolton. (1992). "An Incomplete Contracts Approach to Financial Contracting." *Review of Economic Studies*, 59, 473-94.

Aghion, P., and J. Tirole. (1997). "Formal and Real Authority in Organizations." *Journal of Political Economy*, 105, 1-29.

Bolton, P., and M. Dewatripont. (2005). *Contract Theory*, Cambridge, MA: MIT Press.

Dewatripont, M., and E. Maskin. (1995). "Credit and Efficiency in Centralized and Decentralized Economies." *Review of Economic Studies*, 62, 541-555.

Dewatripont, M., and J. Tirole. (1999). "Advocates." *Journal of Political Economy*, 107, 1-39.

Grossman, S., and O. Hart. (1986). "The Costs and Benefits of Ownership: A Theory of Vertical and Lateral Integration," *Journal of Political Economy*, 94, 691-719.

Hart, O., and J. Moore. (1988). "Incomplete Contracts and Renegotiation," *Econometrica*, 56, 755-785.

Hart, O., and J. Moore. (1990). "Property Rights and the Nature of the Firm." *Journal of Political Economy*, 98, 1119-1158.

Hart, O., and J. Moore. (1999). "Foundations of Incomplete Contracts." *Review of Economic Studies*, 66, 115-38.

Holmstrom, B. (1982a). "Managerial Incentive Problems–A Dynamic Perspective." In *Essays in Economics and Management in Honor of Lars Wahlbeck*. Helsinki: Swedish School of Economics. (See also *Review of Economic Studies*, 1999).

Holmstrom, B. (1982b). "Moral Hazard in Teams." *Bell Journal of Economics*,

13, 324-340.

Holmstrom, B., and P. Milgrom. (1991). "Multi-Task Principal-Agent Analyses: Incentive Contracts, Asset Ownership, and Job Design." *Journal of Law, Economics and Organization*, 7, 24-52.

Lazear, E. and S. Rosen. (1981). "Rank-Order Tournaments as Optimum Labor Contracts." *Journal of Political Economy*, 89, 841-864.

Milgrom, P., and J. Roberts. (1986). "Price and Advertising Signals of Product Quality." *Journal of Political Economy*, 94, 796-821.

Myerson, R., and M. Satterthwaite. (1983). "Efficient Mechanisms for Bilateral Trading," *Journal of Economic Theory*, 29, 265-281.

Noldeke, G., and K. Schmidt. (1995). "Option Contracts and Renegotiation: A Solution to the Hold-Up Problem," *RAND Journal of Economics*, 26, 163-179.

Segal, I. (1999). "Complexity and Renegotiation: A Foundation for Incomplete Contracts." *Review of Economic Studies*, 66, 57-82.

Vauhkonen, J. (2002). "An Incomplete Contracts Approach to Financial Contracting: A Comment." *Economics Bulletin*, 7, 1-3.